The Google Checklist: Marketing Edition 2016

SEO, Web Design, Paid Advertising, Social Media, PR.

Amen Sharma, Paz Sharma & Kavita Sharma

Special Thanks to Gareth James.

HeartCMS.com

Table of Contents

Introduction

The team here at HeartCMS have written The Google Checklist: Marketing Edition 2016 to help you make the most out of your website and online marketing in 2016 and help you take your business to the next level by attracting more customers and generating new leads.

Whether you're a large organisation, a marketing manager or a start-up entrepreneur, we're going to cover everything you need to know in order to have a successful business online.

This book divides into two main sections.

The first section explains everything about creating a Google friendly website. We explain the power of .co.uk and .com domains, how your website should be designed and developed, why your website needs to be mobile friendly, which plugins are the best (and free) and how to keep your website and customers secure with UK Google approved hosting.

The second section of our book explains the world of Online Marketing and how it can be a game changer for any business. We cover everything you need to know on how to rank highly in Google using on-site and off-site white hat Search Engine Optimisation (SEO). How to run your own profitable Pay Per Click (PPC) campaigns on Google and Bing. How to manage and drive traffic to your website using social media platforms such as Facebook, Twitter, Instagram and other upcoming platforms such as SnapChat, and explain how to design your own iOS & Android App.

Technical Skills & Requirements

Most of the guides provided in our book are easy enough to execute with minimal technical skill. While some of the more advanced guides may require FTP & CMS access. We recommend you go over the checklist and allocate as much as you can to your team and if you struggle with the more technical guides give your web developer a call or speak to us for help.

A Free Gift For Our Readers

As a thank you for purchasing this book and to give you a head start with your website and online marketing, we would like to offer you a very special free gift.

We're offering our readers, a free diamond website & online marketing report with a 45 minute consultation with one of our conversion specialist worth £399.

Our Diamond Report includes;

- Website Review by one of our conversion specialist - We'll take a look at your website and give you actionable tips to boost your conversion rate, user experience and search engine rankings. However please be warned: we will be totally honest – we're here to help, so if things need to change we'll let you know!

- Marketing Review - We'll analyse your search ranking and show you which website tweaks and promotion strategies you can implement to boost visibility and bring in more qualified traffic. We will also share tips to boost your social following and engagement. We'll also recommend the best networks for your business, and suggest the type of content most likely to bring you a high ROI.

- Competitor Analysis - If your competitors are doing well online, there's always a reason. We can dissect their campaigns and show you which pieces to copy and which to improve on in order to match – and exceed – their results.

To claim this offer please visit www.heartcms.com/bookoffer

Grammar And Spelling

While we are really good at we do, we are not professional authors. We hope that you gain a tremendous amount of insight from this book through the tips and not the spelling and grammar. We hope you feel we've got this right, although thoroughly checked, it's bound to contain the odd error. We write how we talk and the idea is that it makes the book easy to read. I'm sure we won't be given any literacy awards. We hope you enjoy the book and find it useful.

About Me (Amen Sharma) and HeartCMS

I don't normally talk about myself and my background in my books, however for the first time I've decided to share my experiences. I think it's important for me to do so because some competitors and business owners will look at me and my business and think I've done it, I've reached the top and that i'm successful. Though I really appreciate the comments, it wasn't easy to leave a 9-5 marketing job that paid well, to set up my own business without any tied clients.

It was a real challenge and still to this day I find a new challenge every day. I've been hit by clients wanting things done yesterday and not having the resources to do so, fined by stock image companies for having the wrong license to losing clients because they thought a website without any marketing was enough to appear at the top of Google.

I decided to start my own business after working for a marketing company for around 3 years. I loved my job and I loved the people I worked with, however working 9-5 with a decent pay cheque at the end of the month wasn't for me. I would get home, jump back onto the laptop and work on my portfolio and offer to design free websites to local companies, in exchange for some exposure. I wanted my own business and I wanted to see the day where people would thank me directly for changing their life by expanding their business.

The satisfaction of a customer texting you out of the blue to say thank you is priceless, and to know that the work I have done has helped someone financially is an incredible feeling. People have labeled me as a 'workaholic' and I always answer by saying; is it work if you enjoy it?

The reason I've included this section in this book is because I want you to know anything is possible, if you've just started your business or if you're trying to expand and grow your business, 2016 can be your year. Three years ago I was working a 9-5 job, today HeartCMS have their own in-house team and we're growing day by day.

The key is to educate yourself on what needs to be done and how it's done, then invest your time and money in the right team and watch the results grow your business. Don't be afraid of mistakes, as long as you learn from them and they don't happen again. I just want you to know that success doesn't come overnight and it comes from getting back up when you've made a mistake or you've seen failure but do not give up. In this industry there are all too many self-proclaimed 'experts' who have had little experience out in the firing line. They regurgitate stories about marketing strategies they've never implemented and worries they have never faced. I can truly say I've seen the dark side, lived in moments of worry of having zero clients to establishing a profitable recognised business.

How To Build A Google Friendly Website

One of the most important elements to having a successful business online is to have a Google friendly website. If you already have a website which you've designed yourself or had someone build it for you, there's a good chance that parts of it need updating. The reason for this is because Google wants you to have a dynamic website that's always adapting to the latest trends.

We receive many enquires from potential customers asking us to help with their online marketing, the first action we take is to open and analyse the website. I can confidently say that at least 80% of these websites are poorly designed and built without any consideration of keeping Google and other search engines happy.

The most common issues we find are as follows;

- Website is not mobile friendly
- No contact number visible at the top right of the website
- No quick contact form / request a call back form 'above the fold'
- Top 3 products or services not mentioned 'above the fold'
- No social links
- No Google + account linked
- No eye-catching clickable call to actions
- Slow load speeds
- Have poor ranking domains

… and the list goes on.

The good news is that we're going to cover everything your website needs to be successful in this book (with images), and we're going to update this book every time Google updates its algorithm. So make sure you sign up for lifetime book updates at www.heartcms.com/bookoffer and if you decided to purchase the Kindle version, Amazon will send out a notification every time the book needs updating.

Before we get down to explaining what your website should look like, we feel it's a good idea for you to understand just how good or bad your website maybe with our quick 'Rate My Website' reviewing tool.

You can review your website by visiting www.heartcms.com/rate-mywebsite or by downloading 'Rate My Website' on iOS (iPhones/iPads). Once you've rated your website, keep a note of your score as we will touch base on ratings when reviewing your competitors.

Domain Names

The likely chance of you purchasing this book and not having a domain secured is going to be very slim. However, for our business start-up readers we've included everything you need to know about domains. (If you have a domain and it's not blacklisted by Google, you can skip to Website Design)

When you register your domain name, you'll be bombarded with offers to purchase domain extensions like .co and .blog.

You should be purchasing a .co.uk or a .com domain depending on your location. If you're UK based then we strongly advise to purchase both .co.uk and .com if available, and if you're abroad (USA, Canada etc) then we recommend purchasing a .com domain. We've seen .co.uk and .com's have the strongest relations with Google and other search engines so avoid all other extensions.

Investing in other extensions becomes important only when patenting something or protecting a trademark.

If you're not purchasing a domain with your company name like heartcms.com, then we recommend you purchase a domain with a location or keyword where possible. For example, if you're a gas engineer in London, gasengnieerlondon.co.uk would be a perfect domain.

Check Your Domains History

If you have a domain or are purchasing a new one, it's always worth checking the history of the domain. If you purchase a domain that's expired or has been used in the past, there's a good chance it has a relationship with Google and if it's a bad relationship then you'll want to consider using another domain. To check your domain history, head over to www.heartcms.com/freetools.

Finally, we recommend you register the domain under your own name and address. If an agency is purchasing the domain on your behalf, make sure it's registered under your name and not theirs. The last thing you want is the agency to go bust or fall out with you and getting into a situation of not having access to your domain.

Web Platforms

We're going to briefly touch base on which platforms we recommend you to build your website on. This is important because there are over a hundred options available therefore you are at a high risk of picking the wrong one.

If you have a website then you or your developer have already chosen a platform for your website. However, at times it can be worth changing over to a better platform, as not all are SEO friendly and allow mobile responsiveness (unless you pay extra).

Between us, at HeartCMS we have over 10 years of experience and we have learnt picking a platform for your website can be a vital step to success or failure. Everyday you will see adverts in the papers, on the tv or on Facebook advertising build your own website from as little as...

90% of the time these pre-built services are no good, as they use template based structures that aren't very SEO friendly.

The reason for failure of these prebuilt systems is simple. It's like buying a pre-built car shell and then trying to design a car engine to fit the shell. In an ideal world you would build the engine first and then build the shell around the engine to maximise performance.

Platforms we recommend are WordPress and Magento, but please do not confuse yourself between a bespoke WordPress self hosted install and a free WordPress blog/design on WordPress.com, these are two complete different things.

A bespoke WordPress self hosted site, provides you with the CMS (content management system) of WordPress which saves you lots of time and money. However the front end (also known as the design) is completely bespoke.

Some of the benefits of using WordPress as your chosen platform;

- SEO friendly
- Allows 100% custom bespoke design
- Add unlimited pages to your website
- Use WordPress blog features for no extra cost
- Open source platform giving you access to thousands of pre built plugins and scripts

However, if you're building a large e-commerce site then you have to go with Magento as WordPress is not designed to handle large e-commerce accounts.

Website Design

If you already have a website up and running and you've purchased this book because you're having no or limited success, there's a very good chance it's because your website isn't Google friendly.

If you managed to review your website on our Rate My Website app and you scored below 80, then there's one reason why your website isn't working. We're now going to explain and educate you on how to score 100/100. Not only will this make your website look professional and appealing, you'll find that it will convert your website traffic into paying customers.

This is all important because if you have a website that is not designed for your target audience and Google, it's not worth investing a penny into online marketing. We like to tell all our customers that websites are like cars, and let's be honest we all know a Ferrari or a Lamborghini attracts a lot more attention than a BMW or an Audi.

So it's our job to explain how to get that everyday BMW revamped and running like a 2016 model Ferrari.

Below we've outlined several important design and conversion elements which your website should have.

Mobile Friendly And Responsive

Make sure your website is mobile friendly and responsive - come on, it's 2016. Who doesn't have a mobile device? If your website isn't mobile friendly then you might as well not have a website. Over 1.2 billion people are accessing the web from mobile devices. That's an incredible 80% of all internet users using a smartphone. In other words, if they're online, they are most likely on their phones.

Google favours mobile friendly and responsive sites and with their latest algorithmic updates they have started to penalise sites that aren't mobile friendly. You'll find most social media referrals, links, images and content are also designed for mobile - so supporting these social links are a no brainer.

What makes a mobile friendly and responsive site?

A lot of web designers and business owners think having a mobile friendly website is the same as responsive site. That's actually incorrect, a responsive site is where a website re-sizes for a screen such as an iPhone or an iPad.

Going mobile will likely cost time and money and if your website was created two or more years ago, a new developer might recommend starting from scratch (so you'll be paying for a complete makeover). This is because there are new web development techniques that may make it more efficient to re-do rather than modify your site.

Having a mobile friendly website consists of the way your website looks and works on a mobile and a tablet device, such as the ones listed below;

Keeping calls to action above the fold (the part of the webpage that can be seen without scrolling down) and clear to read. This should include a mobile number that's clickable for mobile devices, social links and a contact form or booking form all above the fold.

Keep menus short and sweet, mobile users don't have the patience to scroll through a long list of options to find what they want. Create a separate mobile friendly menu listing only your products and or services and consider removing additional pages such as about us and testimonials.

Make it easy for the user to navigate back to the home page. Users expect to go back to the homepage when they tap the logo in the top-left of a mobile page, and they become frustrated when it isn't available, or doesn't work.

Make sure your website is developed so it loads as fast as possible, if it takes longer than 3 seconds it's pointless.

If you're an ecommerce site selling products make sure your search feature is visible. Users looking for products usually turn to search, so the search field should be one of the first things they see on your pages. Don't hide the search box in a menu.

Another one for you e-commerce owners, let users purchase as a guest. A study by Google shows that participants view 'guest checkouts' as "convenient", "simple", "easy", and "quick". Users are annoyed by sites that force them to register for an account when making a purchase, especially when the benefit of an account is unclear.

You can also check to see if your current website is considered mobile friendly by Google by visiting www.heartcms.com/freetools.

Make Sure Your Contact Details Are Visible

Advertise your contact number on the top right corner of the website because stats show that this is where 99% of customers look for instant contact details.

If you're a start-up and only have a mobile number, go grab yourself a local or 0800 virtual number, do not use your personal mobile number as your contact number as it looks unprofessional and stats show that website users feel more secure ringing a landline, office or 0800 number.

In your main navigation bar you should have a 'contact us' link and this should always be located last in your navigation/menu bar, this is because stats show this is where everyone looks when looking for a contact page. Some website designers have a habit of hiding the link in the footer.

Also always include as much contact details as possible in your footer, this should include contact numbers, email address and an office address. Having this information visible builds confidence that you're a legit business.

Above The Fold

Above the fold is anything that a user sees once they've landed on your webpage. These are the images, texts, forms and content that is immediately visible without scrolling down. Obviously, there are different folds for different laptop and desktop screens. You don't have to worry about that as much, but focus on the things you want people to immediately see once they land on your page.

Above the fold is uniquely important because it is a new visitor's first impression, but brand familiarity for your returning customers.

What we recommend to advertise above the fold;

- Always advertise your social media icons above the fold. Advertising this helps visitors know you're an established business. Visitors will see your social media links, probably not even click them, but have confidence in your products or services just because you have a social presence.

- Have contact forms (booking forms or free call back forms) above the fold on every single page including your homepage. We split tested the same homepage for a local restaurant using eye-catching gorgeous imagery of food and on the second version we included a contact form titled 'Book A Table'. Such a simple change increased table bookings by 17%. Adding forms can do wonders and this works for every industry.

- Eye catching calls to action. If you want visitors to stay on your website, interact and purchase a product or service, then you're going to have to use some awesome imagery. We always recommend that you use your own images and avoid stock images.

Your own images sell your story a thousand times better than the same stock images found on every other website.

- Sliders, build yourself sliders with your own images and add text above them to build eye-catching clickable sliders. These sliders should last no more than 5 seconds per slider and should be clickable to relevant pages. For example, a Personal Trainer website may be offering '20% off All 12 Week Body Transformation Packages', along with a picture of a female and male keeping fit. Ideally, if this is clicked by the visitor, it needs to take them directly to the '12 Week Body Transformation' page where the user can book or purchase the product.

- Advertise your top 3 products or services so visitors of your website can easily and quickly navigate to the products or services they are looking for.

- Success stories and testimonials, if you can squeeze them in above the fold it's worth mentioning some of the companies you have worked with or customer testimonials. This is another one of them features that help build confidence in your company.

- And of course, all the basic components like your Logo and Navigation.

This doesn't mean that the things below the fold are less important. Below the fold, that's where you put the detailed content. When your visitors are sold on your above the fold impression, they are sure to scroll down and explore the rest of your content.

Killer Content

Having great content is key and always will be. Content is read not only by your visitors, but also by Google and other search engines. It's important to write content that is user friendly, appealing and good for SEO.

For many companies the about us page is the elephant in the room, and often the most awkward thing to write. It's a shame because over the past few years we have seen that analytics often shows the 'about us' page as one of the most visited pages.

The good news is that the 'about us' page doesn't require lots and lots of paragraphs. Many find it difficult to strike the right balance between selling themselves to their customers and driving them away with a self-focused approach, which helps explain why the pages are so often neglected. So we thought it would be great to share a few tips when writing content for your about us page.

Start by talking about your audience, not yourself. Dedicate your opening sentence(s) to your audience's challenges and objectives. Starting with the very reason they come to your website in the first place is a good way to demonstrate that you have their needs in mind and your business is there to help solve a problem.

Present your readers with the facts and figures. This could be anything from your client retention rate to the amount of new products you offer each month to the number of awards you've collected. No one can argue with raw figures.

Let your customers do the talking. When you are thinking of trying out a new electrician, dentist or even a hairdresser, you don't base your decision on what they say about themselves. You turn to those around you. We recommend including several up-to-date testimonials on your about us page, and be sure to include the customer or client's full name and any relevant details that could add credibility to your testimonials.

Include different forms of media. Along with the testimonials be sure to include client pictures to sit next to the relevant testimonials. Make your about us page a feast for the eyes by considering the use of photos, videos and infographics. If people are going to find your about us page, it makes sense to capture their attention for as long as possible and provide them with useful information about your products and services and how you solve the customer's problem.

Also don't be afraid of where you have come from and your history. If, a year ago, it was your business anniversary, celebrate it. The more that people can identify with you, the more trust they'll place in your brand.

Plugins

One beauty about building your website on WordPress is that there are thousands of useful plugins ready made to save you time and money. Plugins allow you to install a piece of code to your website that unlocks new features. We've tried and tested over thousands of plugins and we're going to share the top five must haves;

Backwpup Free

Download your entire website within a couple of minutes and save it as a zip file so you can do weekly backups. We love using BACKWPUP especially if your hosting provider does not offer weekly or monthly backups.

Yoast SEO

Yoast is a must have for all WordPress websites. It allows you to easily customise the meta title and description seen in search engines on each individual page without having to dig into the source code. We will discuss all the benefits of SEO Yoast later in the book.

W3 Total Cache

W3 Total Cache will help your website load a lot faster, it's a great plugin that keeps your visitors what they want as quickly as possible.

Wordfence Security

The last thing you want is all your hard work lost or deleted, especially if you didn't backup your stuff. Wordfence defends your site from nasty all the nasty malware around.

You can download these plugins by heading over to www.heartcms.com/freetools

Hosting & Security

Hosting is very important for any business website. If you're running a business you need fast, secure UK based hosting. The two types of hosting you want to avoid are free hosting and shared hosting.

Free Hosting

The problem with free hosting is that it's free, and free means it's very basic, slow and likely to be a shared server with lots of other unrelated websites.

Shared Hosting

Some shared hosting can be considered acceptable depending on where it's being purchased from. The problem with shared hosting is that your website sits on a server with hundreds of other websites.

Now you may not consider that as a bad thing. However, if on this shared server you have sites blacklisted by Google, this can have an effect on your website just because it's located on the same server.

The ideal hosting you want is either a shared server based in the UK (or US if you're based in US) from a reliable source.

Dedicated Hosting

However for all of our businesses we've always stuck with dedicated servers which means there are no other websites sat on the same server without our permission.

Security

If you're running an e-commerce website or taking payment details over the web, we would personally recommend that you invest into a fast dedicated server from day one and also install an SSL certificate to the website.

SSL allows sensitive information such as credit card numbers, social security numbers, and login credentials to be transmitted securely. Normally, data sent between browsers and web servers are sent in plain text, leaving you vulnerable to eavesdropping. If an attacker is able to intercept all data being sent between a browser and a web server they can see and use that information.

SSL secures millions of people's data on the internet every day, especially during online transactions or when transmitting confidential information. Internet users have come to associate their online security with the padlock icon that comes with an SSL-secured website or a green address bar that comes with an extended validation SSL-secured website. SSL-secured websites also begin with https rather than http. Millions of online shoppers now look out for the padlock when paying for a product or service online, so make your e-commerce website is SSL secured.

Analytics & Tracking Tools

Once your website is up and running you'll want to update it as often as possible. Below we describe all the tools you will need to help you analyse and track your website.

It's important you analyse and track your website as often as possible. Ideally you need to do it weekly. The free tools mentioned will help you learn about your audience, what they like and what they don't like about your website. You then need to use this data to make improvements to your website as soon as possible.

Google Analytics

A free web analytics service offered by Google that tracks and reports website traffic. Google Analytics gets you the data you need to make intelligent marketing and business decisions. It's available for websites, apps, and enterprise businesses.

Once you have Google Analytics installed, you will want to set up Google Goals so every time you receive an email enquiry Google can track data such as date, time, location and the keyword searched by the user. To set up Google Goals, login to Analytics and visit the admin section, then click Goals and follow the instructions.

It's good practice to name your Goals in a way that helps you distinguish one Goal from another. This can help make your Goal Conversion and Flow reports more easily understood.

Webmaster Tools

WMT is another free service offered by Google that helps you monitor and maintain your site's presence in Google Search results. A site that's active in Webmaster Tools has a better shot at being fully indexed by Google. There are also a number of deeper insights from Google Webmaster Tools that can be turned into SEO tactical gold. Once you've signed up for an account, login to the Google Webmaster Tools dashboard. From there, you're able to add your site(s). You'll have to first verify that you own the domain. Google provides verification through an easy pop-up process that allows you to login and verify in just a couple of steps.

Trackable Numbers

We mentioned earlier in the book that one of the website elements you must have is to display a contact number in the top right hand corner of your site. The downfall with advertising a office, local or 0800 number is that every time your phone rings, you don't actually get to find out how your customer found you. Was it a direct visit, a TV or radio advert or a Google search and if so what keyword did they search?

Let's imagine that your business receives 50 calls a month, and let's say 20 of the 50 calls convert into paying customers. How nice would it be to learn what those 20 people had searched on Google before paying you for your products or services. Just imagine what you could do with that information and how it could help you grow your business. With the technology around today, you can get hold of Trackable Numbers (also known as virtual numbers) that gives you access to all the detailed information that's been missing for years. You can find out what keyword was searched to make the phone call, what browser, what device (mobile or desktop), what location and even the day and time.

90% of the websites we design and publish for our clients include a trackable number, the main reason for this is so every month not only can we report what's working but we can stop the methods that don't work and invest money into what we know makes the phone ring.

For more information on trackable numbers visit our detailed page at www.heartcms.com/telecoms/

Now that your website is up to scratch and following Google's latest guidelines it's time to move on to marketing your website.

Online Marketing

We like to tell our clients the truth even before they pay us for managing their marketing campaigns, always remember honesty is key in any business relationship.

Everyone is more than capable of doing their own marketing, be it SEO, PPC or Social, once you understand what to do, actually doing it is quite straightforward and most of it is about performing and repeating tasks. The downfall is, if you want it to be successful, it's a full time job. You can't dedicate a few hours a week and expect to compete against your competitors who outsource marketing to an agency or hire full time marketing managers.

So though it's important you understand anyone is capable of doing online marketing, you also need to invest a lot of time to see the results.

It's important that you understand that if you are going to outsource your marketing to an agency or hire a full time marketing manager, you are still involved because only you understand your industry and business more than anyone else involved. Therefore, you are best placed to identify what your customers need and which of your products and services appeal the most. Your agency or marketing manager should sit down with you before starting any marketing campaigns to understand exactly who your target audience are, what products and services are the most profitable for you and understand what your KPI's are to set up some quarterly targets.

As you're reading this book, we're guessing you've seen someone else benefit from online exposure and you're wanting a piece of the pie.

When a potential customer looks for a product or service online they are likely to use Google. In the UK alone approximately 65% of the population's main search engine is Google. We can also confirm after looking at Analytical data - day in - day out, the vast majority of traffic to websites is from Google organic listings.

The problem is that most business owners think that being on the first page of Google is enough to sustain them and therefore do not invest in any other form of marketing.

You need to understand that once you've managed to get yourself on to the first page of Google, your KPI's should be to keep incoming traffic as high as possible. This is when you will want to introduce marketing such as Facebook & Google Remarketing, this allows past visitors of your website to see eye catching banners on websites such as YouTube, Facebook, Gmail, Hotmail etc for up to the next 90 days or until they convert into an enquiry or paying customer.

Later on in this book we will provide you more advanced strategies for dominating the Google results page. Having stressed the importance of being found at the top of page one. We also want to remind you that appearing anywhere on the first page is better than being lost in the dark depths of pages two and beyond.

Being found online is a game changer for any business and we're about to explain all our working methods so you can achieve these results for yourself.

There are many ways to be found online, and all are as important as each other, below we've briefly described in a short summary all the methods we will be covering in this book;

How To Be Found On Google

The most common focus is Organic Rankings, which is achieved by Search Engine Optimisation (SEO). Organic Rankings also known as Organic Results are the listings that show up in the middle of the page with a white background when you perform a Google search. This area is called organic, because it is not directly paid for.

Trying to organically rank your website will take time, in fact, it can take up to six months depending on the competition levels. The second way to achieve first page on Google is by paying Google directly and appear under the sponsored ads section. This is normally found above and on the right hand side of organic results. These ad's are known as Google Adwords or Google Pay Per Click (PPC).

Google + Local is also known as Google Places and is another way to help index your business into the first page of Google. Google provide more screen space to their map listings than ever before as it becomes more popular amongst businesses who rely on a local presence or physical location. Google has already created listings for many established businesses, and if this applies to your business it is important that you claim your listing as soon as possible and get to work on optimising your listing, with information such as opening hours, contact numbers and an eye catching gallery.

Another way to advertise on Google results pages is to get Google to index your videos (from YouTube) onto the first page of Google. I'll explain how this is done later in the book.

Google Remarketing is another method provided by Google, however, it does not directly advertise your business on Google. Google Remarketing advertises your website using text and banner ads on websites that are linked to the Google network. We will later explain the importance of Remarketing and how to achieve phenomenal results using Google Remarketing.

How To Be Found On Facebook

The most important way to be found on Facebook is by starting off with a Facebook Business (Like) page. It's important you don't create a friends page for your business, as a friend's page does not hold any business value in Google or Facebook's algorithm.

Facebook Videos are another important method of marketing directly on Facebook. If you upload your videos natively onto Facebook, your videos will benefit from features such as auto play back.

Facebook Ads work in a similar way to Google Adwords, you add funds to your Facebook account and then select the target audience you want to reach out to on Facebook. The ad's instantly go live (after a review process) and traffic is sent to your advert and website.

Facebook Remarketing, identical to Google Remarketing but for Facebook. If someone visits your website and then leaves, for the next 90 days they will see eye-catching banners for your website advertised in the newsfeed of Facebook.

How To Be Found On Instagram

With the volume at which Instagram is growing, you'll want to be found on Instagram before your competitors. Using an Instagram account for your business is very important and links well with Facebook adverts. We've seen our clients grow overnight with the use of Instagram. It's important to use hashtags for every image posted, I'll explain why later in the book.

Instagram Ads, because Instagram was purchased by Facebook back in April 2012, it works really well with Facebook Ads and Power Editor. Instagram Ads are fairly new and not many companies have jumped on to the wagon, the sooner you test Instagram Ads for your business the better.

How To Be Found On Twitter

Having a business Twitter page is very important, it can be as powerful as a Facebook & Instagram page. One thing to remember with Twitter is the character limit on each post and to be sure that you use the characters available with the best possible keywords.

How To Be Found On Social

We will also cover some of today's most useful social platforms, including; LinkedIn, Pinterest and Snapchat. We've included a section on these social accounts later on in the book and advised which type of businesses can benefit from these platforms.

SEO (Search Engine Optimisation)

Everyone wants to be on page one of Google, the good news is anyone can achieve page one of Google, but the bad news is it takes time, money and resources.

We like to split SEO into three sections, on-site SEO, off-site SEO and SEO/PR.

On-site SEO is all about improving and optimising the landing pages, content and images on your own website.

Off-site SEO is measuring and improving all the things about your website mentioned elsewhere on the internet such as blogs, articles and social media.

SEO/PR is part of your off-site SEO and it's the things we do to help gain off-site exposure to help create a buzz about your website and influence your rankings.

We like to value on-site SEO as approximately 20% of your overall SEO score and off-site SEO as the remaining 80% of your overall SEO score.

Google use their own algorithms to measure how well your website has been optimised for the following;

- Website's relevance to what the searcher is looking for
- Popularity of the site elsewhere on the net
- Size and profile of the website
- User experience
- Mobile friendliness

- Load speeds

We cover each element later in the book to help you understand how to SEO your own website.

White Hat Vs Black Hat

We don't normally get asked these days about the difference between white hat and black hat and I believe it's because Google has made it clear that your website will be punished if you use any black hat techniques on your website.

That being said, this book is all about marketing and SEO so it's important we briefly cover the rules set out by these search engines. There are a handful of website owners out there that prefer to rank their websites using strategies that are not so Google friendly. However, they use these methods known as black hat techniques because they believe they work just as well and take less time than the traditional approved methods mentioned in this book. Though black hat or spammy techniques can work and rank your website, Google penalise any websites they find using them. We always recommend you stay away from spammy techniques, even if you see a competitor using them - it won't be long before their begging Google for forgiveness.

While it can be tempting to try out some of the dark side techniques and submit your website to link farms which send low quality backlinks to your website, it's not worth it. We receive enquires every other day from clients who have used poor SEO agencies or freelancers that have purchased low quality backlinks and weeks later have been penalised and rankings completely vanished from page one of Google to nowhere.

You'll find that most well established SEO companies stick to white hat strategies such as the ones mentioned throughout this book. If your business really means something to you and you want to dominate Google rankings we suggest sticking to white hat SEO.

On-site SEO

To achieve maximum exposure in the search engines and keep your users happy you need both off-site SEO and on-onsite SEO. In our opinion on-site SEO is just as important as off-site SEO and must be done before you start investing time and money to your off-site SEO. Below we talk about some of the most important on-site elements you need to cover.

SEO Friendly URLS

You want your page URL's to be short and keyword rich. Google has stated that the first 3-5 words in a URL are given the most value. Below we have outlined some good and bad URL examples for a made up personal training company based in London.

Good:
This is a good example because the website has a dedicated landing page for the service 'personal training london' it's not too long and it's not spammy.

http://www.ptfitnesslondon.com/personaltraininglondon

Bad:
This is a bad example because the landing page ranked is the index page, this means Google has not been given enough information to rank a subpage for the service 'personal training london'.

www.ptfitnesslondon.com

Another bad example for you is what we like call 'default links', this tends to happen if you use a template or pre built website. It auto generates links for you;

www.ptfitnesslondon.com/?a192

Spammy link URL

We very rarely see these rank because Google's algorithm avoids spammy links. However, it's worth showing you some examples so you don't get too carried away when creating your own optimised link URLs.

www.ptfitnesslondon.com/personaltraininglondon-londonpersonaltraining

What makes a perfect URL - ideally you want to describe your content in your URL. If a user can look at the address bar (or a pasted link) and make an accurate guess about what the content of the page before ever reaching it, you've done your job. Also remember to keep it as short as possible, don't use numbers or dates and avoid using folders. This means all your product or service pages should be within the root folder so they read /personaltraininglondon and not /services/personaltraininglondon.

Page Titles, Description and Formatting

When search engines are indexing your pages among the things they check include, the page title, the description of the page and the headings.

Page Titles

Each page must have a unique title that will help both search engines and users understand what the page is about.

A page with title "Personal Training London" is better than a page with the title "index.html". Later in the book we will be doing some competitor research to see what titles your competitors are using to rank well.

Descriptions

The page description is what the searcher will see in the search engine results page. So it has to be descriptive, up to 150 characters and unique for each page. It's your opportunity to advertise your page and convince the searcher to click your link and visit your website rather than selecting one of the other links.

Formatting

A page needs to be formatted correctly. Think of it like a report which needs to have a heading (H1) and subheadings (H2). Important parts of the report are highlighted with bold, underline or italics. Do not just throw text on a page for the sake of it, and make sure that it is readable.

Loading Speeds

Google has indicated site speed (and as a result, page speed) is one of the signals used by its algorithm to rank pages. A slow website means that search engines can crawl fewer pages using their allocated crawl budget, and this could negatively affect your indexation and Google rankings.

Page speed is also important for user experience. Pages with a long load time tend to have higher bounce rates and lower average time on site. Longer load times have also shown to negatively affect conversions and online sales.

Amazon found this to be true, reporting increased revenue of 1% for every 100 milliseconds improvement to their site speed. (source:

Amazon). Here are some of the many ways to increase your website's speed;

Image optimisation

Optimising your images is key to improving your website speed. If you edit your own images, then we recommend saving them as web friendly JPG or PNG format. This will help keep your image file sizes as low as possible. If you're using WordPress, and already have lots of images that might not be optimised then you can install the WP Smush.it plugin to automatically compress your images. This will reduce the size of your images without losing any visual quality. The great thing about this plugin is that it works in the background every time you upload a new image. You can also run it retrospectively on all of the images uploaded to your media library.

Use a caching plugin

A Cache plugin allows your website to load faster, if you're using WordPress, one of the quickest and easiest ways to cut your page loading speed is to install a caching plugin like WP Total Cache or WP Super Cache. Both are free to download and very good.

On-Site Relevance

We found one of the key elements Google look for is relevance. Relevance is measured using methods such as;

- Content used on your website throughout it's indexed pages.
- Keyword, Title and Description Tags
- Image files and alt tags (indexed by Google images)

Keywords are another key element in Google's ranking algorithm. The words people search and type in Google to find a product or service are called keywords.

For example 'private dentist nottingham', 'alarm system for bmw' and 'local locksmith' are all keywords.

Building your website pages with optimised keywords is extremely important and accounts towards your on-site SEO. Every page on your website has the ability to rank and attract visitors so it should have its own Title, Keyword, Description Tags and its very own specific content. The keywords that you decide on will depend on your business and the products or services you have to offer.

Short Tail Vs Long Tail Keywords

For Search Engine Optimisation, long tail keywords are becoming more important for small and medium size businesses. The difference between short tail and long tail keywords is simple, short tail keywords are short phrases or keywords, they have high search volume and lots of competition. Where long tail keywords are slightly longer, have less competition and less search volume, but can be easier to rank for.

Typical long tail keywords could contain up to three, four or even five keywords. Being longer, long tail keywords (for example, personal training in london) are used more by users searching for something specific.

Typical short tail keywords are generic keywords (for example, personal training) and have the advantage of driving a lot of traffic to your website. The searches per month for a short tail keyword would be greater than that of a long tail keyword. It would be great for a business to rank for these high volume short tail keyword terms, however trying to rank for these terms can be quite difficult and would take a lot of time, money and resources.

Normally, for short tail keywords there is a lot of competition and are targeted by 'bigger' companies. Most businesses make the mistake to focus on just a list of generic short tail keywords which have high competition levels and then struggle to rank on search pages.

Long tail keywords are the strategy to embark and to start benefiting from traffic through search engines. Targeting long tail keywords can achieve page one rankings within a few months of a good white hat SEO strategy. These types of keywords while having fewer searches will bring more relevant traffic and can help bring higher conversion rates due to being more relevant than short tail keywords.

Keyword Research

Now you're probably asking how to work out what keywords to use and how to check what keywords your competitors are rankings for.

We're now going to explain how to perform keyword research, we recommend you work on an Excel document and have 4 columns and label them as the following; (or download our free ready to use template at www.heartcms.com/freetools)

- Column 1: Products/Services
- Column 2: Competitors
- Column 3: Customer Search
- Column 4: Google Keyword Tool

Preview of what your keyword research document should look like;

	Products/Services	Competitors	Customer Search	Keyword Tool
Keywords				

For this example we're going to say we own a car garage offering Used Cars, MOTS, Car Servicing in and around Nottingham.

For the Products/Services column you will be generating a keyword list, by listing all the products or services your company offers along with the location if your business is a local business.

So for example, our list of keywords for Column 1 would be something like;

- Used Cars Nottingham
- Second hand cars Nottingham
- Mot Nottingham
- Nottingham Mot centre
- Car service Nottingham
- Car servicing Nottingham

Now fill out column 1 with all the products or services your business offers.

Updated preview of keyword research document;

	Products/Services
Keywords	Used Cars Nottingham
	Second hand cars Nottingham
	Mot Nottingham
	Nottingham Mot centre
	Car service Nottingham
	Car servicing Nottingham

For the second column; Competitors, we will need to perform some basic competitor research.

To do this we simply one by one Google the keywords we listed in our Products/Services column and then open the top three organic websites that rank for these keywords.

So for example, I would first google 'used cars nottingham' and then open the top three organic listings. Then we need to find the source code of these three websites, this is done by clicking 'View' or 'Tools' in your browser and then clicking 'Developer' or 'Source Code'.

Once the source code is visible on screen, press CTRL+F on your keyboard to open the find box and then type 'Title'. If the competitor has done any type of SEO (likely as they ranked top three) you will see what they have entered as their title tag. You want to read this and take note of any keywords they have used within the title tag.

Example of a title tag when viewed in source code;

<title>Cars for sale in Nottingham - Nottingham Cars Ltd</title>

Next type 'Keyword' in the find box and note down any keywords the competitor is using and add any useful keywords to your list.

Example of a keyword tag when viewed in source code;

<meta name="keywords" itemprop="keywords" content="used cars nottingham, used cars in notts" />

Finally type 'Description' in your find box and have a read of the description tag the competitor is using and take any useful keywords from this and add to your list.

Example of a description tag when viewed in source code;

<meta name="description" itemprop="description" content="Nottingham Cars Ltd offer a range of used vehicles in and around the nottinghamshire area. If you're looking for used cars in nottinghamshire call Nottingham Cars Ltd today" />

For our example after performing a quick Google search on 'used cars Nottingham' I found a company using the following keywords to add to our Competitor list;

- Cars for sale Nottingham
- Used cars Nottinghamshire

Replicate this task for the other two sites that ranked in the top three positions.

Updated preview of keyword research document;

	Products/Services	Competitors
Keywords	Used Cars Nottingham	Cars for sale Nottingham
	Second hand cars Nottingham	Used cars Nottinghamshire
	Mot Nottingham	cheap used cars nottingham
	Nottingham Mot centre	
	Car service Nottingham	
	Car servicing Nottingham	

Column three is a fun one, we like to call this one 'customer search' and what we mean by this is, what do you think your customers are searching in Google for the services or products you offer.

For our example of a car garage company in Nottingham, we believe customers would search keywords such as;

- By company name (if you're already established) - for example 'Nottingham Cars Ltd'
- Cheap MOT Nottingham
- Cheap car servicing Nottingham
- Used cars Nottingham with reviews
- Cheap used cars in Nottingham

Update your spreadsheet and add these to column 3.

Updated preview of keyword research document;

	Products/Services	Competitors	Customer Search
Keywords	Used Cars Nottingham	Cars for sale Nottingham	Nottingham Cars Ltd

	Second hand cars Nottingham	Used cars Nottinghamshire	Cheap MOT Nottingham
	Mot Nottingham	cheap used cars nottingham	Cheap car servicing Nottingham
	Nottingham Mot centre		Used cars Nottingham with reviews
	Car service Nottingham		Cheap used cars in Nottingham
	Car servicing Nottingham		

Our final column is for Google Keyword Tool, a free tool provided by Google to help you select keywords for Google Adwords. This section of the book explains how to use the tool for SEO benefits, but later in the book we will explain the benefits of Google Keyword Tool for your Google Adwords Campaign.

You can find a direct link to Google Keyword Tool by visiting www. heartcms.com/freetools.

Once you've opened Google Keyword Tools, we want to select the option 'search for new keywords by using a phrase, website or category' and then enter a few keywords.

For this example we're going to enter our keyword 'used cars', then click the 'get ideas' button.

🔍 **Find new keywords and get search volume data**

▼ Search for new keywords using a phrase, website or category

Enter one or more of the following:
Your product or service

used cars

This tool is really powerful because it generates new keyword ideas based on the keywords you want to rank for. Here's a few keywords we'll be adding to column four that we've selected from the results we had with Google Keyword Tool;

- Car dealerships Nottingham
- Car prices Nottingham
- Automobile website Nottingham
- Find cars Nottingham
- Search cars Nottingham
- Car dealers Nottingham
- Pre Owned cars Nottingham

Updated preview of keyword research document;

	Products/ Services	Competitors	Customer Search	Keyword Tool
Keywords	Used Cars Nottingham	Cars for sale Nottingham	Nottingham Cars Ltd	Car dealerships Nottingham
	Second hand cars Nottingham	Used cars Nottinghamshire	Cheap MOT Nottingham	Car prices Nottingham
	Mot Nottingham	cheap used cars nottingham	Cheap car servicing Nottingham	Automobile website Nottingham
	Nottingham Mot centre		Used cars Nottingham with reviews	Find cars Nottingham
	Car service Nottingham		Cheap used cars in Nottingham	Search cars Nottingham
	Car servicing Nottingham			Car dealers Nottingham
				Pre Owned cars Nottingham

You have now generated a list of keywords suitable for your website. If you have time we recommend you look at as many competitors as possible, we normally tend to review at least ten sites to get a good amount of research.

Competitor Lookout

Now it's time to digest your competitors in a little more detail, see what they're doing well and note down anything we can learn from their success.

By doing our keyword research task you should have an idea of what keywords you want to rank for and who your competitors are. We are now going to perform a Google search on all the keywords we found in our keyword research task and populate a full list of competitors.

For this example we are going to change our company from a Nottingham Car Garage to a Personal Trainer in London, this is so we can share as many examples as possible.

Company Name	URL	K1	K2	K3	LL	RMW	Notes

Spreadsheet Cheat Sheet

URL - Competitors URL
K1 - Keyword one
K2 - Keyword two
K3 - Keyword three
LL - Local listing
RMW - Rate My Website Score
Notes - Notes

It's important to perform this task so you know what you're up against for the following reasons;

- You'll learn from competitors who are dominating the online market for your industry.

- You'll learn about the way they advertise themselves, their products and or services.

- You'll see which competitors have signed up and claimed Google Places (as a local listing)

- You'll find some new ways to develop your business by learning from your established competitors. You will notice some competitors offering something for free like a PDF ebook, or free postage on all orders or a free MOT with every service.

The idea of this task is to collect as much research as possible so you want to add as much information to this document to help you understand the level of competition you're up against. This task will also save you time and money because you'll learn exactly what your competitors are doing to rank well.

What We Need To Capture

Company Name - Google the list of keywords you found from the keyword research task and start filling in your competitor's names.

Website URL - It's important to keep the URL in mind, there will be a time you go back to these sites and see how content and offers change on these websites depending on how active they are.

Keywords - We're going to locate the top 3 keywords from each site, sometimes we like to capture the top 5 but for this demonstration we will only capture 3, however if you have the time go for more.

Local Listings - If you're a local company like a Personal Trainer in London then Local Listings are key, you'll want a map to advertise your place of work and this will help your organic rankings. At this stage we want to know which competitors are local and have claimed a Local Listing and we want to separate these from the bigger organisations.

Rate My Website Score - Earlier we talked about finding out the score for your website and how it's rated with the latest Google requirements. We're going to do the same with your competitors and see how well they score. You'll find websites with a score of 80 or above are likely to have been professionally built by someone or a group of people who understand Google, SEO, Design & Development.

Notes - This is where you go crazy and add all the additional little bits of information you find. This can include things such as Call To Actions used and additional services offered like Live Chat.

Fill out the first two columns, here's an example of the document filled out for a Personal Training company in London.

Company Name	URL
PT Fitness London	www.url.com
Keep Fit London	www.url.com
Personal Training London	www.url.com

Now to find the Keywords being used by your competitors, we're first going to go on to each websites and look at the competitors source code.

Remember the 3 things we are looking for are;

- Keyword Tag
- Title Tag
- Description Tag

Here's an example of the keyword tag for a personal trainer website in London;

<meta name="keywords" itemprop="keywords" content="pt sessions in london, personal training london, 12 week body transformation london " />

Here's an example of the title tag for a personal trainer website in London;

<title>Personal training london - PT Fitness London</title>

Here's an example of the description tag for a personal trainer website in London;

<meta name="description" itemprop="description" content="PT Fitness London offers 1-1 personal training in and around London. All of our personal trainers are qualified and have over 5 years of experience in personal training. " />

Update your spreadsheet once you've picked out useful keywords from the keyword, description and title tags.

Updated preview of competitor lookout document;

Company Name	URL	K1	K2	K3
PT Fitness London	www.url.com	personal training london	london personal training	personal trainer london
Keep Fit London	www.url.com	keep fit london	personal training london	north london fitness
Personal Training London	www.url.com	pt sessions london	personal coaching london	london personal coaching

Now to check if the websites have a Google local listing. To check this perform a Google search on the company's name or a keyword you have found them rank for and see if they appear on Google maps like the example below.

If the competitor appears and shows as a local listing type yes, and if not type no.

Company Name	URL	K1	K2	K3	Local Listing
PT Fitness London	www.url.com	personal training london	london personal training	personal trainer london	yes
Keep Fit London	www.url.com	keep fit london	personal training london	north london fitness	no

Next, we need to find out the score of these websites using Rate My Website via our iOS app or by visiting www.heartcms.com/ratemywebsite.

Company Name	URL	K1	K2	K3	Local Listing	RMW Score
PT Fitness London	www.url.com	personal training london	london personal training	personal trainer london	yes	70/100
Keep Fit London	www.url.com	keep fit london	personal training london	north london fitness	no	30/100

Now to add any additional notes we've found while researching these websites.

You want to keep an eye out for the following;

- What makes them unique (are they offering an incentive for using them)

- Do they have any reviews using review tools such as TrustedReviews.com or TripAdvisor.co.uk

- Do they offer a live chat service

Here's an example of our updated document after adding some notes;

Company Name	URL	K1	K2	K3	LL	RMW	Notes
PT Fitness London	www.url.com	personal training london	london personal training	personal trainer london	yes	70/100	appears more than once for Personal Training London, has a youtube video appear in Google when searching for personal trainer london.

We usually repeat this exercise for at least 5-10 competitors and at least 5 keywords, remember the more information you have the better understanding you'll have of the competition.

The point of this task is to understand which companies are your main online competitors. At this stage you should have found there are several different companies ranking for the keywords you want to rank for. These may include local competitors you've heard of before along with bigger organisations or online retailers.

Competitor Study

Now that our Competitor Lookout document is filled up, we want to select three of our biggest competitors. You should know who your biggest competitors are by this stage and if you struggle to select three, we recommend selecting the small/medium size companies that appeared to rank rather than the online retailers or big chain companies. If you offer a niche service like 'Pet Sitting' you may find you only have one or two competitors, if this happens then work with the sites you've found as these are your only online competitors.

Now that you've hand picked your top three competitors, we're going to study them and find out how to outrank them. Now it's time to create 3 more tabs called 'Study 1', 'Study 2' and 'Study 3'.

The information we will be studying is how these three competitors market themselves, in what context and how well both on-site and off-site SEO is optimised.

The study of our competitor websites will include looking at;

Organic Listings - We want to look over the organic listings (advert) in the Google results page and analyse the title, keywords, url and description used by your competitors. This will help us understand how our competitors are talking to Google & their target audience.

We will shortly include good and bad examples of organic listings so you understand how to manage your own on-site SEO meta tags.

Landing Pages - Once we've analysed the organic listings, we're going to click the adverts and check over the landing pages. We will show you how to analyse these landing pages from a design and conversions point of view and also show you how well these websites have been optimised for SEO so you know what you're up against.

Content - We will be checking over the content of all three competitors. Content is key and always has been, business owners tend to miss the value of content and write very short spammy paragraphs. I will show you how to write killer articles for your website and blog.

Website URL Structure - We will show you how to check if your competitors are using optimised URL strings and if they are creating separate hidden pages for Google to index.

Backlinks - As mentioned previously, having quality Google approved backlinks are a big part of a successful marketing campaign. I'll show you how to find out what backlinks your competitors have and how you can get some quality links for your website.

We're going to start off by picking our first of three competitors;

Once you've picked your first competitor, you want to head over to Google and search for their top/first keyword (which was found while performing our Competitor Lookout task).

For example;

Google   personal training london   🎤 🔍

You then want to locate where the site appeared in Google and study the Title, Description and URL used.

(organic listing designed for demonstration only)

Personal Trainers in London & London Personal Training
www.weburl.co.uk/**personal-training-London** ▾
Local **personal trainers** in **London** with award winning qualifications. **Our Personal Trainers in London** provide a great way to get fit and are all insured and ...

Title = Personal Trainers in London & London Personal Training

URL = /person-training-london

Description = Local personal trainers in London with award winning qualifications. Our Personal Trainers in London provide a great way to get fit and are all insured and...

You want to copy this information into your Study 1 document tab;

Company Name	Web URL	Google Rank	Title	Description	Link
PT Fitness London	weburl.com	1st place	Personal Trainers in London & London Personal Training	Local personal trainers in London with award winning qualifications. Our Personal Trainers in London provide a great way to get fit and are all insured and...	/person-training-london

This task is important for you to understand how your top ranked competitors are talking to Google. As you can see from the advert preview above, Google auto highlights in bold any related keywords within the advert that match the users searched keywords. This helps increase Click Through Rate (CTR) to your website as it shows the user relevance to the search they have performed. You can see this is a good advert as the title includes the searched keywords, the URL includes a destination of the keywords searched and the description highlights the service and location keeping the entire advert Google friendly and 100% relevant to the user's search.

Here's a few examples of other types of organic listings you may come across, we're showing you these so you understand what makes a good organic listing and what information you should be using when building your own Meta Titles, Keywords & Description Tags.

Good examples;

This is a good example because the Title, URL and Description talks about the service the company offers, and because Google robots have indexed this information as relevant to the searched keyword it is likely to rank well.

Personal Trainers in London & London Personal Training
www.weburl.co.uk/personal-training-London ▾
Local personal trainers in London with award winning qualifications. Our Personal Trainers in London provide a great way to get fit and are all insured and ...

Here is another good example, this one includes everything as the above advert but also includes a Call To Action (CTA) in the description 'We offer a free consultation for new customers'.

Looking For Personal Training in London
www.weburl.co.uk/londonpersonaltraining ▾
We have the very best personal trainers in London offering 1-1 personal coaching and bespoke nutrition plans. We offer a free consulation for new customers...

Bad examples;

This is a bad example because the Title is using the company name, which isn't likely going to include the keyword or location of the keyword. For example if your company is called Keep Fit Ltd and this is your title tag, Google see's no relevance with that heading when a customer searches for personal training london.

Also, because this website has no page called 'personal training london' and all the information is stored on a webpage called services, Google has decided to show the services page as the destination URL. This is bad because a potential customer looking for personal training london is likely to click an advert with a URL advertising /personal-traininglondon over an advert that simply says /services.

You can also see the description of this organic listing is really weak. Though it mentions personal training, it doesn't mention the location next to the keyword. The description is also really short and Google allows you to use between 150-160 characters, so it's best to use up as many characters as possible.

Company Name Ltd
www.weburl.co.uk/services ▾
I offer **personal training** and have over 50 cleints in **London**

Here's another bad example

The title in this advert does not mention the location, which will enable this advert to be outranked by other adverts that mention both service and location within the title. The destination URL has no specific page, this is likely because the owner of this website has not created a separate page advertising the services and has filled all the information about personal training london and the other services they offer all on the homepage.

Also the description used in this listing is by far the weakest, as there is no mention of the actual service or the location.

Google prefer website owners to create specific pages for each product or service (we will go over this shortly)

Personal Training Services
www.weburl.co.uk/ ▾
Company Name Ltd offer fitness plans and 1-1 coaching for both males and females.
Call us for free expert advice...

Here's an example of an over SEO'd listing (also known as black hat SEO).

Personal Training London, London Personal Training, Person...
www.weburl.co.uk/**personaltraininglondon-londonpersonaltraining** ▾
We at personal training london offer personal training in london. We are the best london personal training company around.

Websites like this may rank highly for sometime, however Google will penalise these black hat methods and they will eventually fall away as more and more users will begin to avoid these types of URLs.

Now that you understand how Google works in regards to Titles, Keywords & Description tags - also known as part of on-site SEO. You're now going to click these organic listings and see how well the landing pages have been optimised.

You should have already checked how well these website are optimised for conversions and if they have a user friendly design. You would have done this while doing the competitor lookout task and hopefully ran each competitor through Rate My Website. If you haven't already, it's important to know the RMW score of these three competitors.

Updated preview of study 1 document tab;

Company Name	Web URL	Google Rank	Title	Description	Link	RMW Score
PT Fitness London	www.weburl. com	1st	Personal Trainers in London & London Personal Training	Local personal trainers in London with award winning qualifications. Our Personal Trainers in London provide a great way to get fit and are all insured and…	/person- training- london	70/100

Now we need to find out how well the website's landing page is optimised for the keyword we searched on Google. To do this it's important you read the content in fine detail to see how well the page is optimised for the keyword. For example if 'personal training london' is one of your keywords, you then need to search for this keyword on the landing page and see how many times (if any) it's been mentioned. This can be easily done by reading over the content or by pressing CTRL+F and searching for 'personal training london'. Do keep in mind Google robots are very clever and they will filter keywords written in different formats and phrases. For example, you may find this page only mentions 'personal training london' once. However, you may find that 'london personal training' is mentioned three or four times and they may have mentioned 'london personal trainer' and 'qualified personal trainer london'. These all count so take note of all the possible variations and update your study document.

You then will need to keep an eye out for any headings using the keywords. Headings or Titles within content are also known as H1s, H2s and H3's (heading one, heading two etc) and Google likes it when website owners relate headings to the content and keyword. So in theory a website with an H1 heading of 'Personal Training London' is likely to rank better than a page with an H1 heading of PT Fitness London.

Check over all the headings on the website's landing page and update your study document with the relevant information.

We also want to see how many times the keyword is mentioned behind the scenes, for this we're going to open the source code of this landing page by clicking 'View' or 'Tools' and then 'Source Code', then hit CTRL+F and type in the keyword and see if it's been mentioned anywhere else. A well optimised site would have used it in the Title, Description, Keywords, H1 and Image ALT Tags.

Here's an example of a good optimised image for the keyword 'personal training london'

```
<img src=" http://www.weburl.co.uk/images/personaltraininglon-
don.jpg" alt="personal training london">
```

Updated preview of study 1 document tab;

Company Name	Related Landing Page	H1 optimised	Content optimised	Image Alt Tags
PT Fitness London	yes, it took me straight to a page where I could see they offer personal training in london	yes, H1 heading was 'Personal Training London'	Personal training london was found 6 times on the landing page	image tags mentioned personal training once

You then want to take note of any Call To Actions (CTA) used - this will help you learn from your experience and established online competitors. You might find that as soon as the landing page loads they have an eye-catching banner that says 'first personal training session free' or a 'FREE nutrition guide with every PT session'. If a competitor who ranks highly is using a Call To Action, it's likely because they know it works. You want to expand on these ideas and see what you as a business can offer for your very own Call To Actions.

Updated preview of study 1 document tab;

Company Name	RMW Score	Related Landing Page	H1 optimised	Content optimised	Image Alt Tags	CTAs Used
PT Fitness London	70/100	yes, it took me straight to a page where I could see they offer personal training in london	yes, H1 heading was 'Personal Training London'	Personal training london was found 6 times on the landing page	image tags mentioned personal training once	they offered a free 15 minute personal training consultation

Next you want to see how well the competitors have structured and optimised URL's.

We've already provided examples of good, bad and spammy URL links, here is a reminder of a good URL;

http://www.ptfitnesslondon.com/personaltraininglondon

If you find a similar URL to this one. Then the competitors website is likely to have been optimised. It's important to note done in your document the landing page URL so you can compare these with the other competitors you will be researching later.

Updated preview of study 1 document tab;

Company Name	H1 optimised	Content optimised	Image Alt Tags	CTAs Used	Landing Page URL
PT Fitness London	yes, H1 heading was 'Personal Training London'	Personal training london was found 6 times on the landing page	image tags mentioned personal training once	they offered a free 15 minute personal training consultation	/personaltraininglondon

Finally, we want to check out what backlinks your competitor has and if they hold any value. It's pretty easy to find out what backlinks they have by running a backlink checker on the URL. Visit www.heartcms.com/freetools and find the backlink checker tool and enter your competitors details.

If you currently have your own website and you've done some marketing in the past it's worth checking your own score just to compare.

Once you hit search, the tool will search the major search engines and after a few seconds you'll see a report of how many links the website has, what anchor text has been used and the PageRank value of each link.

Anchor text is the clickable text in a link, when using anchor text be relevant to the page you're linking to, rather than generic text. The keywords in anchor text are one of the many signals search engines use to determine the topic of a web page.

A good example of using anchor text for a link should look like this;

We also offer personal training in london at competitive prices. (note personal training in london text has been hyperlinked to a landing page)

A bad example would be; We also offer personal training in london click here for prices. (note that 'click here' is linked to a landing page).

Remember when checking backlinks you will want to check both the www.weburl.com and weburl.com (without the www.) as websites with and without www. are seen as completely separate sites to most of the Internet.

Now you have this information from our free tools update your study document;

Company Name	CTAs Used	Landing Page URL	Backlinks	Top 3 Anchor Text Used
PT Fitness London	they offered a free 15 minute personal training consultation	/personaltraininglondon	109	personal training london london personal trainers personal coaching london

Now that's only one of your top three competitors done, replicate these steps for your other two competitors. Once you've completed this task you should have an excel document full of information on your competitors that's going to help you come up with your marketing strategies.

Build Your Own Meta Tags

Now you know what your competitors are doing to rank well in Google it's time to come up with your own Title, Description, Keyword meta tags and URL strings.

If you downloaded our template earlier you should have another tab called 'Meta Tags' if you did not download our template you need to make a new tab with the following structure;

Page Name	URL	SEO URL	T Tag	D Tag	K Tag

Spreadsheet Cheat Sheet

Page Name - Name of the website page you're optimising
URL - The current URL of the page
SEO URL - SEO friendly URL
T Tag - Meta Title Tag
D Tag - Meta Description Tag

K Tag - Meta Keyword Tag

We're going to continue to use our example of a personal training company in London, the first thing you need to do is fill in the 'Page Name' column with all the products and services you have to offer.

Here's our updated spreadsheet:

Page Name	URL	SEO URL	T Tag	D Tag	K Tag
Home					
About Us					
Personal Training					
Nutrition Plans					
Fat Loss					
Gallery					
Testimonials					
Contact Us					

Now it's your job to use all the collected information to decide on what URL's and Meta Tags you'll be using.

Below we've filled in the homepage meta tags to give you an example;

Page Name	URL	SEO URL	T Tag	D Tag	K Tag
Home	/index	/index	Personal Training London - PT Fitness London	PT Fitness London offer personal training services in and around the London area at competitive prices.	PT Fitness London, Personal Training, London

Another example for a subpage that offers a service;

Page Name	URL	SEO URL	T Tag	D Tag	K Tag
Personal Training	/page2	/personaltraininglondon	Personal Training London - London Personal Training	Personal Training services in and around London. All our PT's are fully qualified.	Personal Training London, London Personal Training

Google typically displays the first 50-60 characters of a title tag, or as many characters as will fit into a 512-pixel display. If you keep your title tags under 55 characters, you can expect at least 95% of your titles to display properly. Keep in mind that search engines may choose to display a different title than what you provide in your HTML. Titles in search results may be rewritten to match your brand, the user query, or other considerations.

Content is Key

Now that you've planned out your pages, meta tags and looked over your competitors it's time to write killer content for your web pages.

The key when writing content for your website is to make it user friendly, if it makes sense to a real person then it will make sense to Google. Do not over kill it with spammy techniques and don't over-stuff your keywords.

The first step to writing killer content is to keep in mind the specific keyword or phrase that this page is designed to represent. For example if you were writing for the website page 'personal training london' you would definitely make sure page title is Personal Training London.

You would then work on your H1 heading tag, and you would use any useful information from the competitor research task to come up with some good heading ideas. For example, a good H1 could be 'Find Your Personal Trainer in London' which would be followed by a few paragraphs explaining your service 'personal training london' and why they should choose you over your competitors.

You could then add another heading (H2) to make it easier for Google to understand your webpage. Our H2 for this example could be 'Why Choose PT Fitness London' and it could be followed by a paragraph and a few bullet points on why PT Fitness London is the company to choose.

Remember to mention your keyword throughout the page, and remember to match it with your meta tags, page descriptions and page URL.

Replicate this for all your website pages so all the content on your website is well written, unique and relevant to each product or service you are trying to promote.

When writing content for your website it can be tempting to copy text between two or more pages.

Unfortunately, Google doesn't like duplicate text and actually penalise websites which contain duplicate text, whether it's text copied from other websites or text copied from other pages on the same website.

Blogging

It's hard – if not impossible – to succeed at content marketing without creating blog posts on a regular basis. Every successful website has a blog that holds a solid foundation of content, but it's consistency that's the real key to success. According to HubSpot, marketers who are consistent with blogging are 13 times more likely to get a positive ROI.

Blogging is an inbound marketing strategy that truly works. You can generate more qualified leads through blogging on your website than from a radio advert you might pay thousands of pounds for. If your website does not have a blog then we would highly recommend getting a self hosted WordPress blog as soon as possible.

Below we share our top on-site blogging tips;

Reverse Engineer Your Content Creation

Posting articles daily is simply not going to help, the articles you post need to be valuable and informative. You need to write content that attracts more links, shares and comments from others.

To do this, you simply need to reverse engineer your content creation strategy. Instead of writing posts without thinking twice, it's better to create content that is proven to work.

We explain the 3 simple steps to reverse engineering content:

Finding content related to your industry - You can use tools such as Buzzsumo for finding share-worthy high valuable content in your industry. Buzzsumo is one of the best tools out there to help you come up with amazing content ideas.

Using Buzzsumo type in an industry related keyword or topic and find articles written in the last 24 hours which have a high number of shares and likes.

For instance, let's say you run a 'landscape maintenance' business - here is how to use Buzzsumo to find content that gets more shares and links.

With one of the articles reaching over 19,500 shares, you can see from this screenshot that content and blogs about 'ideas' and 'tips' in this industry get the most likes and shares.

Go ahead and open several articles and have a read of them and find one you like.

Make it your own - Once you've found an article that's performing well and relates to your business, you'll want to re-write it and add your own experiences and make it your own.

For example, if this article states that one of the best ideas for keeping low maintenance is by *'Creating a clean border along your flower beds to help prevent weed growth'*. Then you need to elaborate and explain why you agree or disagree with this statement and include any personal experience you may have experienced on this topic.

Reach out to get it trending - Once you have created your own content on your blog, it's now time to reaching out to the right people in your niche.

Here's how can you find out the people who are interested in promoting your content using Buzzsumo. When you enter a keyword on

Buzzsumo, it shows you who linked to the top content including the social sharers by clicking view backlinks and view sharers.

5 Best Low Maintenance Plants That Should Be In Your Landscape
hubpages.com - More from this domain
Aug 4, 2015
Article

% View Backlinks

👥 View Sharers

<❤ Share

Take note of all the backlinks and reach out to them. Connect them on social media, find out their emails and start creating a buzz for your new blog post.

Use attention grabbing blog post titles - Having a catchy title is the key to grabbing people's attention. It's your golden ticket to increased traffic and wider audience.

You need to elicit interest, emotion, and curiosity in your potential readers to make your blog post title as irresistible as possible. This also plays a crucial role in improving your search ranking of your blog post and other related pages.

For example, let's say you're writing an article about your accountants business and your target audience are new start up businesses , instead of using "Starting A New Business" as a blog title, you would want to write "How To Start A New Business in 3 Easy Steps" or "How To Start A Business in Less Than 20 Minutes".

Not only are these titles more attractive, but your post also has a higher chance of landing in the first pages of results since it's more specific. There's less competition for longer titles which are better known as long tail keywords. Checkout our free '100+ Blog Post Title's That Work' cheat sheet for you to download at www.heartcms.com/freetools.

Use Eye Catching Photos

Every blog post should contain a mix of content. Give your articles life by Including your own eye catching images.

Promote Your Blogs on Social Media Sites

If you want to boost your overall website traffic, publish your new blog post on social media sites like Facebook, Pinterest, Twitter, Google+ etc. (We go into a more detailed social media plan towards the end of the book)

Submit to social bookmarking sites: Digg, StumbleUpon, Delicious – all are social bookmarking sites that have huge readers. If your post does well on these sites, take it for granted that your overall search traffic will also increase overtime.

Rich Snippets

Back in 2009 Google decided to add rich snippets to their search results helping users find more information on a large variety of subjects including people, food recipes, events and reviews. Google put rich snippets into place to help website owners advertise their content better, and giving users as much information as possible before they made the decision to click through to a website.

Over the last few years Google have added many more types of snippets to their armoury including products, videos, music info, restaurants, business organisations, people and authors.

Using rich snippets on your website has many benefits including drawing a searcher's attention away from a competitor's listing to your own listing. In turn, increasing click through rate (CTR). This can also lower bounce rate as the user has more information about your business before clicking through.

Adding rich snippets to your website is fairly easy. However if you're not using a CMS system such as WordPress, you may need to hard-code the snippet to your website. We've explained how to do this on our FAQ's page as at www.heartcms.com/faq. If you're using Word-Press, head over to www.heartcms.com/freetools to download the free plugin to get started.

Sitemap

Sitemaps serve as a way to communicate directly with the search engines such as Google, alerting them to new or changed content very quickly and helping to ensure that the content is indexed faster. You'll want to make sure you have a sitemap for your website and then you'll need to open a free Google Webmaster Tools account to submit the sitemap.

Creating a sitemap all depends on the platform your website is built on (WordPress, Magento etc). If you're using WordPress you can find free plugins that generate a sitemap for you, we have the latest Google approved plugins at www.heartcms.com/freetools

Off-Site SEO

Once you've worked on your on-site SEO (approximately 20% value of your overall SEO) you'll want to move on to the off-site elements. However, it's important to check back and keep an eye on Google Analytics to see if your on-site SEO needs any revisions or changes based on the data collected in Analytics. Unless you're receiving over 10,000 visitors a month, you will want to collect approximately 3 months worth of data from Google Analytics before making any changes to your on-site SEO and website layout.

Now that your website is being indexed by Google for the on-site SEO elements that have been worked on, it's time to maximise exposure and work on the off-site elements.

Off-site optimisation is the process of promoting your website across the web. The purpose is to build brand awareness, improve rankings in search engines and attract visitors from 3rd party websites. It's an ongoing process and not a one-off, it needs to be worked on weekly to see results. The best approach to off-site SEO depends on the industry you're operating in and your budget. However, we will discuss an overall strategy that works and what off-site SEO elements should be covered.

Off-Site SEO Checkup

Before we explain what off-site SEO elements need to be worked on it's important to understand what relationship your website may already have with Google and other search engines.

Check your backlinks to your domain or specific web pages are important. The more inbound links you have, the higher your overall Google

PageRank, right? Close, but not quite… Google, and other search engines that matter, reward quality over quantity.

Some website owners and internet marketers try to cheat the system by purchasing a large quantity of backlinks for a really cheap price. As mentioned above, this is known as black-hat and Google can and will penalise your website for using such methods.

Google prefers natural backlinks, and if Google detects low quality backlinks to your website it can affect your rankings. Basically it's better to have 1 quality backlink than to have 10 low quality backlinks.

If your website has been live before purchasing this book, it's worth checking to see if you have any backlinks and if any of them should be a concern.

To do so, visit www.heartcms.com/freetools and click the free back link checker.

Google Approved Backlinks

The first task ahead of us for off-site SEO is to find and capture some Google approved backlinks. There are many ways to do this and we will be looking at;

- Google approved directory websites
- Article submission
- Blogging & Guest Posting

Directory Websites

The quickest and easiest source of gaining backlinks is from Google approved directory websites. When looking for directory websites you will find free and paid ones available. Submitting your website on Google approved directory websites is useful for the follow reasons;

1. As long as the directory site is Google approved, and your website listing is optimised there's a good chance the backlink will help push your rankings up in Google.

2. Some directory sites actually rank well in Google, so not only will your own website rank for relevant keywords, you'll find that some of your directory listings rank below your own website.

You will notice that the free directory websites also offer paid listings, these paid extensions usually involve a promise for more exposure or a 'featured' ad. Our personal recommendations are to avoid the paid listings as we are using the directories primarily for Google credit and not traffic directly from the directory site.

Below we've outlined a few tips to make sure you optimise your listings for maximum Google credit;

- Make sure the title includes your business name and location. For example if you offer personal training in Swindon make sure the title reads; Company Name - Personal Training Swindon. If you're a national company, try include product or service names. For example, Company Name - Award Winning Personal Training.

- For your description make sure you mention your business name, keywords and locations, but most importantly make sure it's readable and doesn't look spammy.

- If the free directory allows you to add a link back to your website then make sure you use a keyword as the anchor text and link it back to the index page of your website.

- If the free directory site allows you to add media such as images, videos, testimonials, and opening hours, then take full advantage of this and fill them all in.

- Make sure your contact details are exactly the same as the contact details you've entered in Google places / Google +.

Industry Specific Directories

While searching for directory sites or using our Google approved list at www.heartcms.com/freetools, you will likely find industry specific directory sites. These specific sites are very useful and can help with Google credit, we've seen that particularly post Google Penguin update, that Google gives importance to links from websites that are targeted and relevant.

The best way to find a good directory site is by performing a Google search for each of your keywords and looking for directory listings in the results. If the directory site is ranking in Google, it's likely to be Google approved.

Another method to find good Google approved directory sites is by running the backlink checker tool on your competitors sites and seeing what directories are being indexed.

It's important to note that there has been plenty of talk on blogs and forums about Google penalising websites who seem to get a high number of links in a short period of time. However, because most Google approved directory sites require a manual approval (for them to get in touch and try and upsell to a featured listing), if you are to spend a day or two creating directory listings do not worry about it too much as all listings will get approved at different times.

Avoiding Automatic Listings

Like most online marketing tasks, you'll find yourself repeating yourself on each directory site. We know it can be quite tempting to look for a piece of software that might automate this for you (because they do exist), however from past experience, we recommend that you manually submit your listings so each directory is optimised as much as possible.

The automated software we have seen does not offer the level of accuracy and optimisation a listing requires for it to be effective.

Avoiding Spammy Backlinks

You'll find thousands of websites offering 'high quality' backlinks and directory submissions. While these services can seem extremely good and cheap because of the fake testimonials or a good looking checkout page, they all use automated software for submissions and use the same description over and over again. This can be flagged by Google as duplicate content and your website can be penalised and rankings can be effected. You'll also find these 'high quality' directory sites are no good and are already blacklisted by Google. Stick to manual submissions and either use our updated Google approved directory sites or one's found ranked highly by Google.

Article Submission

Another way to gain Google approved backlinks to help your rankings is by writing and submitting articles about your products or services around the web.

We recommend article submission as one of your backlink strategies because you can often get your articles submitted on websites with higher authority than directory sites.

For example, if decide to write an article on '10 ways to keep fit at home' you can submit the article to sites such as ehow.com. Google likes these websites because they generally hold high value content and information.

Like directory sites, you will find many low end article submission sites, and these can easily be identified by checking to see if your article is submitted without a manual approval. If the site allows article approval automatically it's not worth using.

When submitting an article make sure it's unique and not posted elsewhere. Do not use online 'spinners' or rewrite your article by changing a few headings. When we say each article needs to be unique, we mean unique.

This may seem like a long process, but if you want good long lasting results you have to follow Google's rules and each article must be rewritten and not posted over and over again.

Guest Blogging

You've probably heard by now that having a blog on your website is great and if you do a blog post now and then it'll help you rank higher in Google... broadly speaking this is correct. However, it takes good content and time to see page one results.

Guest blogging is where you write an article and approach another website owner that runs a business within your industry that is willing to blog about your website.

The first challenge with guest blogging is finding someone willing to post your article. The truth is many websites now have a blog and many website owners struggle to write or find good content for their own blog. So as long as your article is well written and will be valuable to readers, website owners will snatch the the well written article out of your hands.

We always find that surveys, competitions, giveaways and free advice articles are much more likely to get attention.

Remember the idea of guest blogging is to gain a backlink from another website, so make sure your website is somehow linked within the article. We always find it best to have an 'about the author' section below the article and have that section mention your business name and website. It's obviously great if you can get a link within the article around relevant content, but don't compromise the quality of your article by making it look spammy.

Optimising Videos

With Google's recent updates they often include videos within its search result pages, and unless you're in an industry where a lot of your competitors use video, it's unlikely that they will be using this strategy to try and get more exposure on the first page of Google.

Did you know that video content already makes up 64 percent of all internet traffic, according to Cisco's 2014 Visual Networking Index, and it's forecast to grow to 80 percent of all traffic by 2019. The popularity of video has spread to advertising and marketing, as well, with eMarketer estimating that $7.77 billion was spent on online video advertising in 2015.

The presence of video itself affects the most important SEO ranking factor (content). Video is evidence of quality content and helps send signals to search engines that your website contains rich media (videos) relevant to search requests. It is expected that search engines will continue to increase the ranking factor of including video as consumers demand video in search results.

Creating and optimising videos on platforms such as YouTube, Dailymotion, Viddler and Photobucket have many benefits including more exposure on the first page of Google.

Not only are well optimised videos indexed by Google but they rank completely separate from your normal organic rankings. Which means if your website is new and nowhere to be found on Google, a quick way to see rankings appear on page 1 of Google is by uploading and optimising videos.

Lots of business owners avoid making videos because they think they are time consuming, expensive or don't really know what topic to make a video on. You can easily get promotional and explainer videos created and published for as little as £100, or you can grab a camera and a blank wall and film yourself talking about your products and services.

For example let's take Dollar Shave Club's promotion video that went viral. The video cost approximately £3,000 and generated 12,000 orders within 48 hours. That was four years ago; today, the video has almost 20 million views.

When optimising your videos make sure you use keyword rich descriptions, titles and mention locations if you're a company offering local services.

While shares and links to your YouTube video won't count as backlinks to your website, you can create two backlinks from a YouTube account. Create a YouTube channel and add your website page into your channel's profile. Also insert your link in the video description.

In addition to creating videos and uploading them to video sharing websites such as YouTube, you'll want to embed these videos to your own website. Google and other search engines tend to like videos and in particular like videos that show relevant titles and descriptions to the landing pages of your website.

Once your videos are uploaded to the video sharing sites and embedded in your website, you want to get more people to like or view your video by sharing it on your social channels, this is a positive signal to search engines of the value of your content. This will increase the likelihood of your video being found and driving traffic to your site.

Exclusive Tips For YouTube

As mentioned above, for the best results you'll want to add your videos to as many platforms as possible including YouTube, Dailymotion, Viddler and Photobucket.

However as you're probably aware, YouTube is owned by Google, and YouTube is the world's second largest search engine, and it has the least competition for eyeballs across all social platforms. To put this in contrast, here is a few snap shots of the same search terms competing on Google and YouTube;

Question, which of the two (Google & YouTube) do you think is the easiest and quickest to get a first page ranking on? Yes you guessed it, Youtube.

You may ask... Why aren't more people creating videos to go after YouTube rankings? It's a combination of a fear of looking bad on video, the unwillingness to spend a day figuring out how to create a decent video, and wanting to hide in anonymity through a web page.

What most people don't seem to realise is that you can remain anonymous behind a slideshow or screencast, and it takes half the time to create a video as it does a blog post.

Now we've given you a perfectly good reason to start creating videos for your business, we are going to give you some killer tips that work wonders.

Target Keyword Phrases

When you're doing your keyword research try to aim for words that have a minimum of 500 monthly searches. Although YouTube is the second largest search engine, it pales in comparison to Google. Going after a lower searched long tailed phrase is usually a waste of time and resources.

Use The Keyword Phrase Directly In The Filename

When saving the filename for your video, be sure to include the keywords separated by hyphens. This filename is read by YouTube's/ Google's algorithm, and it can increase your chances of ranking higher.

If you were trying to show up for the keyword phrase "Hair Salon Nottingham," then these are some good and bad examples of filenames.

Bad filename - video12324.mp4

Optimised filename - hair-salon-nottingham.mp4

Know What Types of Searches Google Automatically Uses Videos For

We all know when we're looking for a tutorial or a how to, we're normally presented with videos on Google's search results.

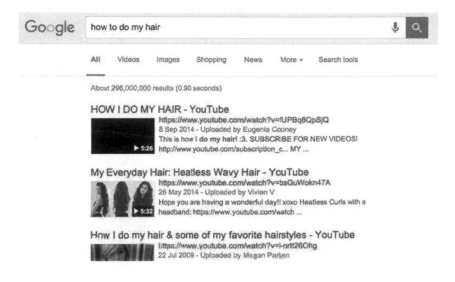

By creating videos with these keywords, you have a better chance of ranking on Google's front page in addition to YouTube.

Create a Keyword Rich Description with Over 250 Words

Your video descriptions are just as important as your titles when it comes to YouTube SEO. It is vital to make sure your description has at least 250 words and include the keyword 2-5 times.

Link to A Related Blog Post in the First 15 Words of the Description - Over 40% of people that watch the entire video will click on the link in the first part of the description. Here are three ways to double that number:

- Create Targeted Content - A big mistake most business owners make is just sending them to their home page. If your video has tips about 'how to do your hair', then create a blog post to support the video and link it in your description.

- Use an Annotation Call to Action - Create a call to action annotation within the bottom part of the video that points to the link. For example you can write, "Click the url below to see my blog post on doing your own hair."

- Ask Them to Click - At the end of each video ask them to click on the link in the description to see the great related content in your blog post.

YouTube keeps track from the moment they start watching your video and until they hit the back button. If viewers go to your blog post after they watch the video, then it increases the average time on video. This is another key factor in determining YouTube rankings. If they stay on your video page longer than the competition, then you will outrank them.

Create Eye-Catching Thumbnails To Draw In A Wider Audience

The thumbnail is the image that is displayed to people before they click on your video. In essence, it is a mini advert to draw people in. Be sure to use the most colourful and vivid shot from your video to gain the biggest audience possible.

Engage Your Audience to Increase Your Comments & Shares

Comments and shares are another key factor in the YouTube SEO algorithm. Here are the best ways to increase the number of comments on each video.

- Ask a Question at the End - Simply say something like; "How did I do?, Did you find the video useful? Please provide me some feedback in the comments below."

- Offer to Answer Questions - Most people watching your video will think you are an expert on the topic. Offer to answer any questions they have in the comments section. You can take this a step further by offering a freebie or incentive to the person that asks the best question.

- Respond to Comments With Questions - By asking your commentators questions, it can create a discussion that can lead to more comments and new clients.

SEO/PR

The success to an SEO/PR campaign is to generate awesome content marketing. It may seem like an impossible thing to do, but with a bit of research you'll find a topic that's trending and easy to talk about.

Content marketing is essentially a way of communicating with potential customers considering to purchase your products or services and is a strategic marketing approach focused on creating and distributing valuable, relevant, and consistent content to attract and retain a clearly-defined audience — and, ultimately, to drive profitable customer action.

Content marketing comes in the form of text, images, infographic, tweets, sound files and even video clips, pretty much anything that can hold a value and a message.

The idea is to create content that's going to help promote your business by providing something in return such as a giveaway, competition, free product or even a discount.

The idea of teaching instead of selling seems to turn marketing on its head, and yet it's at the core of content marketing. "Teach, don't sell" is exactly what makes content marketing different from advertising.

If you think your business is too small to need a PR campaign, think again. Every business has a public image which reflects what people think about them and why people choose to do business with them.

It's important for every business to have a PR strategy because, it sets you apart from your competitors and makes your brand the voice of the industry.

Before a potential customer buys into your business whether it's a product or service they are likely to check your 'public image' before doing business with you. Your public image is made up of all the visible information about your business on the web, which includes; social media comments, likes, shares, reviews, testimonials and blogs.

When a potential customer comes across your business and makes a decision to purchase a product or service from you, it will be hugely influenced by what they see that others have said about your business online. For example, take a teenager, young adult or a homeowner who wants to find an electrician, they won't be looking in the local newspaper or the big yellow book. They'll be using Google, and once they've found an electrician they'll be looking for reasons to use or not use them by looking out for reviews and comments.

SEO/PR does just that, it helps your potential customer find all the good things that have been said or put forward about your business in Google search results.

Understanding The Goals of An SEO/PR Campaign

Below we discuss the four main goals set out to be achieved from a SEO/PR campaign.

Build A Database

One of the reasons we suggest having an SEO/PR campaign is to help build a database and then using the database to increase sales.

Creating a database of existing and potential customers is something that every business should be doing at every opportunity possible. As discussed in our website design section of this book you should have a 'sign up to our newsletter' section on your website. However, this section of the book is about building a database with the use of content marketing.

The difference between a 'sign up to our newsletter' section on your website and building a database using content marketing is that with content marketing the potential customer might not even be on your website, and is using the content visible elsewhere to signup or give you permission to sign them up.

Increase Website Traffic

We all love the sound of more traffic to our website, because we all know traffic = leads, and leads = sales.

We will be explaining how to develop an SEO/PR campaign to drive more traffic to your website and how to influence this traffic with the use of Google & Facebook Remarketing.

Build Brand Authority

One of the main reasons we suggest running SEO/PR campaigns are because they help build brand authority. There's nothing worse than losing a new potential customer because they saw a bad review about your business on the first page of Google. Now we're not saying it doesn't happen, because one day one client will decide to write up a bad review about your business because of a bad experience, it happens. What we need to do is make sure the potential customers see the good reviews because at the end of the day, it's your job as a business owner to make sure all your customers are satisfied with your services or products.

The idea of an SEO/PR campaign is to make sure Google indexes all your content and good reviews to the first page of Google.

Increase Sales And Traffic

The most obvious goal is to receive a return on investment and improve sales. The methods of measuring a successful SEO/PR campaign are broken down into two sections;

If you see an increase in traffic to your website from the SEO/PR campaigns you're doing something right. (Remember traffic = leads and leads = sales)

Conversion Rate

You'll find that the traffic to your website from an SEO/PR campaign holds a stronger conversion rate then your normal SEO organic traffic. This is mainly because the content you have fired up is 100% relevant and will only target a mass audience of people look for your products or services.

Identifying Your Target Audience

To create successful content for your SEO/PR campaign, you need to know and understand your audience. Not every business has a product or service for everyone, you may be running a business for a hair beauty salon and you already know that your audience is primarily females, or you may be a local builder and know your audience are people within a 25 mile radius of your business or home.

There's a host of elements that need to be considered when identifying your target audience and this will include, age, gender, location, marital status and their requirements.

Below we explain how to identify your target customer and build a look and feel to present killer content.

How to Identify Your Target Customer

Grab a note pad and pen and start to scribble down who you believe is your target customer.

Start off with demographics and note down an age bracket, gender, education, job title, income and marital status.

Example: Online Fashion Retailer.

Demographics:

Age Bracket : 16-35
Gender : Primarily females
Education : University graduate
Job Title : Part Time / Full Time worker
Income : Over £5,000
Marital Status : Single

Once you've built your target customer demographics, you'll want to build up your target customers interests;

Example;

Interests:

Shopping
Likes to blog, likes to shop at brands such as Asos.
Always on their phone.
Partying at weekends.
Holidays.

Once you've built your target customer interests, you'll want to build up your target customers goals and dreams;

Example;

Goals and Dreams:

Wants to walk on red carpet premieres.
Get free products to review for their blog.
Attend fashion events and tour the world.

And finally you'll want to work out how your product or service benefits your target customer;

Example;

How Your Business Helps:

We provide quality fashion at competitive prices.
We provide a 14 day refund policy (try before you buy)
We provide XS and XXL clothing unlike our competitors.

By performing this exercise you'll be able to fully understand the problems and needs of your target customer and this will help you build great content for your SEO/PR campaign.

Selecting A Topic

When deciding the topic of an SEO/PR campaign, it's not as simple as picking up an idea that you've seen elsewhere or just something you want to try. Don't make the mistake of thinking an SEO/PR campaign is all about you and your business, it's not! It's about appealing to your target customer and solving a problem.

After years of running successful SEO/PR campaigns we found the following discussions help create awesome topics:

- What is your most profitable products or services?
- What are your main business objectives?
- What does your target customer do on a daily basis?
- What is your USP?
- What are the leading companies in your industry talking about?
- What is trending and how does this link to your business?

Remember that any content you come up with for your SEO/PR campaigns will need to appeal and provide something to the target customer. This is not an advert, this is a PR campaign. An advert doesn't need to hold value or a free attachment, an SEO/PR campaign does.

How To Find Trending Topics

It's important to research topics, ideas and trends to help you create a strong SEO/PR campaign and you can do so by finding the following tools by visit www.heartcms.com/freetools.

Google Trends - This free tool analyses a percentage of Google's web search history to figure out how many searches were done over a certain period of time. It allows you to find out what keywords are trending and how the trend has changed over time and even predicts how the trend may change in the future. For example, if you search for 'Fashion' in the UK, Trends analyses a percentage of all searches for 'Fashion' within the parameters set and provides valuable data on trending topics such as London Fashion Week and The Brit Awards.

Twitter - By accessing Twitter's now trending page you can see the top trending keywords and influencers within your industry. Perfect for IT related companies, local plumbers, builders and the likes.

Instagram - Very similar to Twitter, it allows you to see what Instagram accounts and keywords are trending. Perfect for fashion companies, beauty salons and the likes.

Pinterest - Great place to look for ideas and inspiration, with other users pinning to ideas every few seconds it's a great place to get creative ideas for your SEO/PR campaign. Perfect to find infographics.

Buzzsumo - Great site that shows you what articles are currently trending. Perfect to see what content is being shared and liked online.

Here's a few snapshots of our findings for our Online Fashion Retailer;

The Brit awards

Search interest in hosts Ant & Dec

London Fashion Week AW16

UK search interest in London Fashion Week

Interest over time

Let's break down the points mentioned for our Online Fashion Retailer;

What is your most profitable products or services? - All of our new arrivals are profitable products and we have lots in stock.

What are your main business objectives? - We're trying to be the next big online fashion retailer for females aged between 16-35.

What does your target customer do on a daily basis? - They spend time blogging about fashion and beauty products, partying at weekends and enjoying a movie night with friends.

What is your USP? - Unlike many other online retailers we provide XS all the way to XXL and provide a full 14 day money back guarantee.

What are the leading companies in your industry talking about? - Always talking about student discount.

What is trending and how does this link to your business? - The Brit Awards, where all fashion role models attend. London Fashion week, all beauty and fashion bloggers attended this event.

By doing this exercise, we've gathered enough ideas to build a strong SEO/PR campaign;

- Try to link to London fashion week or Brit awards
- Provide something for bloggers
- Organise a party or an event
- Student discount promotion

For the sake of this book, we're going to look into the idea of 'providing something for bloggers'.

However below we've outlined a few points for the other ideas that we came up with;

- Try to link to London Fashion week or Brit Awards - If we decided to use this idea we could offer tickets to the next fashion event and talk about the trending topics from London Fashion week.

- Organise a party or an event - We understand our target customer likes partying and fashion events, why not host an event for our online fashion retailer. Customers attending are presented with a welcome pack which includes discount codes and free samples.

- Student discount promotion - A great way to grab attention in the world of digital PR is by offering a discount. If you're already offering 10% student discount why not offer 16% for the week of Brit Awards 2016 and create a new voucher code called 'BRIT16'.

Create A Title For Your Campaign

Now that you understand your target customer, and have a topic for your campaign - it's time to come up with an attractive title.

The example we've used for the purpose of this book is an online fashion retailer.

For this campaign we've come up with a title 'SnapChat Tricks Fashion Bloggers Will Love'.

Note, that we've built the look and feel for this campaign by breaking down our target customer information:

Campaign title: 'SnapChat Tricks Fashion Bloggers Will Love'

The reason we've come up with this title is because our target customer is likely to be a blogger and we want to give them something for free. In this case we have decided to provide some free 'tricks' for SnapChat, a social media app used by millions of fashion bloggers.

The goal of this campaign;

- Get published in fashion related websites, newspapers and magazines.
- With an attractive title, the article should get read and shared by many fashion bloggers and SnapChat users.
- Gain new followers and customers.
- Generate traffic to the website.
- Increase sales.

Getting Your Campaign Heard

Now that you've come up with an awesome SEO/PR campaign idea, it's time to find ways to get it published before you write it. That's right, before you write it. You'll want an idea of where your SEO/PR content will be placed so you know what type of look and feel, tone and language you will need to use when writing your content.

You may be asking why you can't host your own article and post it as a blog or publish it on a Facebook brand awareness campaign. The truth is you can, however, if you're a new business with a new website or drive very little traffic to your website then nobody is going to see your campaign.

Though we highly recommend blogging on your own website as often as possible, your excellent SEO/PR article should be placed onto a different website, perhaps a local/national newspaper site or a well known blog site in your industry.

Imagine if your article 'Snapchat Tricks Fashion Bloggers Will Love', gets onto a fashion bloggers website with over one million followers and a discussion started about their favourite Snapchat filters. If your article can start a discussion online, then more and more people will be talking about your article and this will lead to more and more traffic for your website.

Having said that, it's always good to have a re-written snippet of the article on your own website once it has been published by a third party website. It's important you stay away from copying and pasting it for a few reasons, once the article is published make sure that you re-write a snippet of the article and not just copy the first paragraph or two.

Building A List of Target Publications

There are over a million websites that accept good content and articles, but the challenge is getting your content published on a website or magazine that has the right audience for your business.

We get many of our clients asking us to get featured on high profile websites such as Forbes, New York Times or The Huffington Post. You need to remember the reason you've spent so much time coming up with great SEO/PR content is to reach out to your target audience, and not just to get listed on a high profile site with a completely different target audience.

To help find a list of publications for our campaign we're going to use the same tools we used to help us find a topic.

The three main tools we use are to help generate a list of target publications are Google Trends, Google News and Buzzsumo.

Go ahead and open Buzzsumo, and type in one of your primary keywords or type in the topic you're going to write about. We also recommend changing the filters to show 'past month' only.

For our example of a online fashion retailer, we started off by searching 'fashion';

Once you see results related to your industry you'll want to do the following;

- Click the article post and check to see how related the site looks for your target customer.
- Check how many shares and likes the article gets - the sites with more likes and shares are the ones you want to target.
- Click view shares and see what influencers have shared the article.
- Check the number of backlinks on the website URL by checking it on opensiteexplorer - this will allow you to check to see if the site has any spammy backlinks.
- Copy the website url into quantcast.com and check to see if you can locate the demographics to make sure it fits your target customer demographics.

Screenshot below shows some of the key elements to check on Buzzsumo;

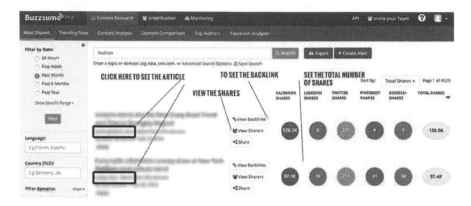

Screenshot below shows the demographics information collected from quantcast.com;

Once you've collected a handful of target driven high authority websites from Buzzsumo and checked the demographics using quantcast.com, you'll want to start looking at other ways to build your list of target publications.

Using Google To Build Your Target Publication List

You can pretty much find anything on Google, and finding target publications using Google couldn't be easier.

The two Google tools we recommend are Google Trends and Google News (both can be found on www.heartcms.com/freetools).

Simply perform a Google News search (by visiting Google, and clicking the 'news' tab) and search for your keywords or article topic and see what target publication sites rank well and feature well written content. You'll find some sites ranked are the same high authority sites found on Buzzsumo, but don't be shy to visit page 2 of your results to see what other sites you can add to your publication list.

Local Publication Opportunities

If you're a local business offering your products or services just to a specific location, you'll want to lookout for what we call 'local publication opportunities'. The easiest method we've established to find local publications are;

Your local newspapers, most cities in the UK have their own local newspapers, and every newspaper company no matter how big there are - tend to have a website. The easiest way to find all your local newspaper companies is by performing a Google search on '{location} newspaper', for example Nottingham newspaper. Any newspapers you find are worth adding to your publication list.

Local Magazines - most UK cities have local magazines that help promote local businesses, and many of these local magazines tend to have websites. You can find these by searching for '{location} magazines'.

Local Business Blogs - by performing another Google search you'll be able to find some highly ranked blog sites with good authority and traffic.

Check Your Local Competitors - if you have a competitor in the same area, copy their URL into open site explorer and check to see if they have any backlinks from local newspapers, blog sites or magazines.

Now that you have a list of target publications to pitch to, we're going to share our methods on writing a perfect SEO/PR article. We'll then show you the best ways to pitch your article to your target publications.

Building Great Content

Now that you've noted down your target customer, created a title for your campaign and have an idea of your target publications, it's time to build great content.

As previously mentioned content marketing comes in many different forms. It can be an article, a blog post, infographic, e-book, video, sound file or even an audio book. Understanding which content marketing platform is best for each campaign is a vital part to its success.

When deciding on how to build the content for your campaign you will want to consider;

- How old the target customer is
- Their gender
- Where are they based
- What device they are using
- The voice of your brand

These elements are important because you have to remember that a potential 16 year old female browsing on a mobile device is going to consume the content differently to a 30 year old male browsing on a desktop.

Let's break this down by coming up with a content marketing plan for our example 'SnapChat Tricks Fashion Bloggers Will Love' for our online fashion retailer.

- How old the target customer is - We already know our target customer is aged between 16-35.

-   Gender - We know our primarily target customer is a female.

-   Where are they based - Our online fashion retailer targets the UK.

-   What device they are using - Looking at Google Analytics, 75% of shoppers are using a mobile device and only 25% are using a desktop or laptop.

-   The voice of your brand - We'll be pitching our article as a fashion expert.

There's so many different possible ways to generate great content that we're going to focus on what we believe is the top two methods; written content and creative artwork. If you would like to learn more about our case studies and other types of SEO/PR content give our blog a follow.

Why design creative artwork for your SEO/PR campaigns - More than any written content, an image or video is a shareable piece of content. Studies show that Facebook photos get 39% more interaction than written content, and videos are an opportunity to draw people in with good, well-developed storytelling.

The only downside with creative ads is that you're likely going to have to hire a graphic designer if you want the job done correctly, and though creative ad campaigns can become viral overnight it's still possible to get the same attention from a well written article.

How To Write A Perfect SEO/PR Article

As we previously mentioned SEO/PR is about teaching and not selling, but you're probably asking isn't the whole point of marketing to sell? If you're not selling, are you even marketing?

Even when you're creating educational content, you are still marketing. You're just marketing the content instead of marketing your products and services directly. You're still selling those products and services, but the selling is just way in the background. Way, way in the background. Let's take our example of 'SnapChat Tricks That Fashion Bloggers Will Love' - in no way does anyone see this blog linking to an online fashion retailer trying to sell clothes. Why? because the point of your marketing – your content marketing – is to build an audience that consumes and shares your content.

Here's the part you might not like hearing. You teach instead of sell, because frankly, nobody really cares about your marketing. Sorry to tell you that, but it's true. Nobody wants your marketing. We're all up to our ears in advertising and marketing. We see over 2,000 ads and brand messages per day, and our potential customers are starting to develop an issue known as 'banner blindness' - that's why it's so essential to teach, rather than sell.

It's also at the essence of how content marketing can be so effective, like this book for example. The point of content marketing is not to swamp people with ads or pitches; it's to give useful, relevant information.

Tips To Help You Write A Perfect SEO/PR Article

Select a handful of categories and tags that explain your article - It's worth provide categories or tags for each article you write, this will website publishers dictate the target audience.

Upload a featured image - Pictures say a thousand words, using a featured image for your article that related to your content.

Open the article with a powerful paragraph - If you're educating the user or providing something for free make sure this is mentioned as soon as possible.

Include videos, images and infographics where possible - Sometimes just plain text can be boring and throughout this book we've explained how videos are taking over. Include a video or infographic in your articles when possible.

Don't include a call to action that asks them to buy - You've done so well to understand your target customer, write a perfect article - don't downgrade your article by adding call to actions to your products or services.

Example of our published article for our online fashion retailer.

The screenshot below shows; the title, author's name, date published, categories and tags.

Snapchat Tricks That Fashion Bloggers Will Love

   👤 Amen Sharma Ⓢ February 24, 2016 📁 fashion, snapchat, blogger, fashion blogger, tips and tricks,

The screenshot below shows; the featured image / thumbnail image;

The screenshot below show snippets from the article;

You probably don't want to leave your phone on the wrong date for too long, or it could mess with all sorts of things, so when you're finished snapping, change the time back to automatic.

4. Give your snap a playful tint

This one blew my mind: you can use an emoji to give your snap a colorful sheen. Choose an emoji of the color you're interested in, then make it so large (by expanding with two fingers) that it covers the entire screen. Move it around until a transparent edge of the emoji allows your image or video to peek through.

How To Pitch Your Campaign

Now that you've got an amazing article and a target publication list, there's only one person that can stand in your way, an editor.

You now have the task ahead of you to convince editors that your campaign is going to be successful and useful to their customers.

Learning how to communicate with editors is an essential skill and can take time to master.

Below we breakdown the changes of pitching your campaign;

Find The Editor

You've already built a target publication list, now it's time to find the editors. The simplest method we found is to navigate through the publication's website and look for a meet the team or contact us page.

Try and find the editors information, even just a first name can be useful as you can go scouting on social media channels looking for their profiles. Once you've gathered all the contact information of all the editors you want to target, it's time to pitch your article to them.

The Pitch

The make or break part of the process, you need to do more than just send an e-mail.

As expected an editor can easily receive hundreds of emails in a day, so it's your job to make sure your pitch (email) stands out from the rest.

You have full control over your pitch, so it's best to plan and take your time before sending out that deadly e-mail. You've got to remember that the editor is time restricted and wants the campaign to benefit the publication. As long as your pitch nails the unique selling point and benefits to the publication within 60 seconds of the editor reading the pitch - you've got half a shot of getting the deal.

The Email

It's time to draft up an attention grabbing email. You probably won't be surprised to learn that most journalists and editors prefer email pitches over phone calls. You also may not be surprised that there is a lot of conflicting advice about how to make your email pitches resonate.

The subject line of your email is our first challenge. If the subject line draws the attention of the editor, there's a good chance that your email will be opened.

It's best practice to keep your subject line as clear as possible, so we would recommend mentioning 'story idea', 'editorial submission', 'press release' or 'interview opportunity' after the main subject line.

The next challenge we need to master is to make sure the editor reads the e-mail once its opened. This requires a good headline and exclusivity, make sure the opening title and paragraph states exactly what the editor wants to hear. By providing exclusivity to your article, you'll have a far better chance of sealing the deal.

Check your grammar and don't attach any files. If there's anyone that's going to judge you on your ability to put together an article, it's an editor. Also we recommend that you link your article using something like Google docs rather than attaching the article as a PDF or document. Attaching a file increases the likelihood that an email will be sent to the editors spam folder.

SEO/PR Case Studies

Here's a few case studies of content marketing and SEO/PR campaigns our team have ran and have been very successful;

Case Study One

Our first case study comes from a local Indian Restaurant wanting to gain more social media awareness and increase table bookings for valentines compared to last year.

Once we we're given the objective our research team went away and presented the idea of providing a how-to video to make the restaurant's famous red and pink cocktail at home.

We filmed the video for our client and produced the content for the article, published it and measured the campaigns success via social media likes, shares, comments and table bookings compared to last year.

Client Industry: Indian Restaurant.

Objective: Brand awareness, gain YouTube views and subscribers and gain table bookings for valentines.

Target Customer: 18-40, in a relationship, likes indian food.

Article Format: Written recipe with embedded YouTube how-to video.

SEO/PR Title : Valentine's red and pink cocktail recipe.

Categories & Tags : valentine's, cocktails, romance.

Featured Image:

Results:

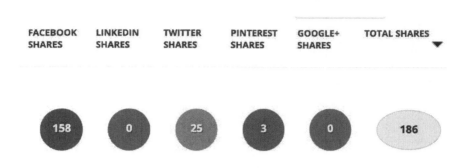

FACEBOOK SHARES	LINKEDIN SHARES	TWITTER SHARES	PINTEREST SHARES	GOOGLE+ SHARES	TOTAL SHARES
158	0	25	3	0	186

Now you maybe thinking 186 shares is nothing, let us remind you this was for a local Indian restaurant and thanks to this PR stunt they reached out to an audience they would have never attracted with advertising. With the help of this campaign the restaurant received an increase of table bookings of 13% for valentines day compared to 2015.

Case Study Two

Our second case study is from a campaign we ran for a UK car dealership with multiple branches.

We we're given the objective to promote their new service of 'fitting car winter tyres'. Our research team went away and presented the idea of providing a how-to guide on 'Winter is coming - checking your car before setting off'.

Client Industry: UK Car Dealership.

Objective: Promote new service of 'fitting winter tyres for all makes and models'

Target Customer: 18-40, car owner, UK audience.

Article Format: Written how-to guide, with infographics on road accidents caused by bad weather.

SEO/PR Title : Winter driving - how to check your car before you set off.

Categories & Tags : cars, car owner, safety, winter, winter checks, road accidents

Featured Image:

Results:

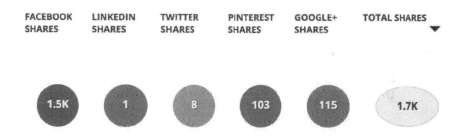

Finding Influencers To Promote Your Business

You might know them better as Bloggers, YouTubers and Celebrities. These influencers are trusted voices who can bring in customers and help you build your community. They're capable of exposing your message to a target audience by posting content to their loyal followers on your behalf.

Influencers are constantly getting pitched by marketers, making it all the more important for you to stand out from the crowd if you want them to pay attention. It's well worth investing time in building connections with high quality influencers and turn them into a brand advocates who will be willing to help you out over and over again.

Using Google To Find Influencers

A great places to start finding influencers is by performing a simple Google search. For our example let's look for fashion bloggers for our online fashion retailer.

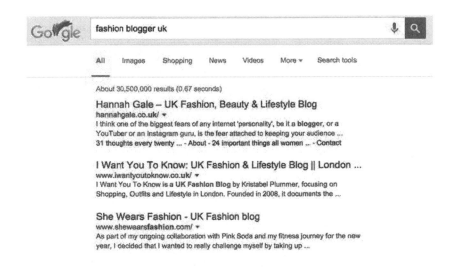

If a blogger's website is ranking on the top three pages of Google, you'll want to contact them and ask them to work with you to promote your brand. The likely chance of them ranking highly for such a broad keyword is because they are seen as a high profile influencer by Google.

Research Influencers In The Right Niche

Don't just look for influencers with the biggest following and pick them. If your product or service isn't relevant to their audience, their

PR won't benefit either of you. Search for bloggers who might share the same audience as you're looking for.

You can use Google search to find influencers for any type of industry, influencers are not always linked to fashion. Below we've highlighted a few examples to give you an idea on how easy it is to make this relevant for any business;

If you run;

- A travel agent or currency exchange business - search for 'travel blogger'.
- A local beauty salon - search for 'beauty blogger in {location}'.
- A local restaurant business - search for 'foodie blogger' or 'restaurant review blogger'.
- A pet shop - search for 'dog blogger'
- A car dealership - search for 'automotive photography blogger'.
- A interior design business - search for 'interior design blogger'
- A personal training - search for 'fitness blogger'

You'll want to note down all the top influencers you find, you can download our free 'influencers' spreadsheet from www.heartcms.com/freetools or make a quick spreadsheet like the one below.

Name	Web URL	DA	BL	IF	AIER	TF	ATER

Spreadsheet Title Cheat Sheet

Name - Influencers name
Web URL - Influencers website link
DA - Domain authority
BL - Backlinks
IF - Instagram followers

AIER - Average Instagram engagement rate
TW - Twitter followers
ATER - Average Twitter engagement rate

The information you'll want to collect includes;

- Influencers Name
- Website URL
- Domain Authority (found by doing a quick 'opensiteexplorer' search)
- Number Backlinks (found by doing a quick 'opensiteexplorer' search)
- Social Media Followers
- Average Engagement Rate

Here's an example of our spreadsheet filled out.

Name	Web URL	DA	BL	IF	AIER	TF	ATER
Amen	amensharma.co.uk	30	1,304	12,042	7.2%	8,325	6.6%

Using Klear.com to find influencers - Find and create relationships with the top influencers in your sector and build your community.

Find Influencers

You'll want to note down all the top influencers you find into your spreadsheet.

Using Instagram to find influencers - A nice easy way to find instant trending influencers on Instagram is by doing a basic search using the Instagram app.

You'll want to note down all the top influencers you find into your spreadsheet.

Hopefully now you have a list of high profile industry-related influencers that you can pitch too.

We'll now explain how to use these high profile influencers to help promote your brand.

3 Ways Influencers Can Work With Your Brand

Sponsored Posts

This is when an influencer is paid to write and publish a blog post in their own style which mentions and includes a link back to the brand's website. This normally includes the blogger to post your product/service review on their social media channels.

The Advertising Standards Authority (ASA) regulations state that a blogger should include a disclaimer that the post was sponsored by the brand and there will usually be a short line at the end of the blog post stating this.

Product Reviews

Sending products or providing your services to an influencer in exchange for a review on their blog and some social media coverage gives you an excellent ROI. A business could send an influencer a product such as clothing or a service such as online fitness plans, and ask them to write about the product or service.

If the influencer loves the product or service, they will definitely say so in their review and this will lead to great online exposure for your business.

Giveaways

A great way to boost social media followers and gain website traffic is by offering a limited time competition. All you need to do is provide an influencer with two products, one for them and one for a lucky follower.

Ask the influencer to host a competition on their blog and social media sites, where one lucky winner will be entitled to winning the second free product.

Pitching Your Brand To Influencers

There's many ways you can pitch to an influencer, you can try direct emails, direct messages on Instagram or even send them a quick tweet about your offer. However, if you've ever attempted to pitch to high profile influencers you'll notice that they don't tend to read direct messages because of the amount of spam they get and direct e-mails can be missed.

Below we share you our tips on pitching to influencers that work.

Make them notice your name - You need to start a relationship with the influencer before pitching to them. You could do this a few days or even hours before sending out your offer.

Here are a few things you could do:

- Comment on their latest posts - Make it long and thoughtful and credit their post.
- Tweet their latest posts and @mention them.
- Follow them on social media channels and like some of their most common posts.

These few extra steps will make them notice your email. So when you email them, your name stands out from the crowd.

Use An Attention Grabbing Subject

When it comes to emailing an influencer, using a powerful attention grabbing subject can be the difference between your e-mail being opened or dumped into the spam folder.

We've seen many brands and even PR companies send out generic emails to a hundred plus potential influencers and hope for as many replies as possible. We all know by sending out hundred e-mails you're likely to get one to two responds but they won't be the high profile influencers you want.

We recommend each email you send out to be specific for each influencer you target, and though you can reuse parts of the pitch the intro and conclusion should be tailored for each influencer.

Below we share a handful of bad and good pitch examples;

Influencer Outreach E-mail For A Clothing Brand - Bad Example

Subject used: Review Our Product

Dear Jessica, I am writing to you about an opportunity to work together with our fantastic brand. We would be really pleased to let you work with us on our exciting new fashion brand. We're sure that you and your followers will love our trending fashion products! You can email me back and let me know if you are interested.

Speak soon,

Amen.

Influencer Outreach E-mail For A Personal Trainer - Bad Example

Subject used: Keep fit with my plan

Hi Jessica, How would you like to work with me and my company for free?

Please let me know if you're interested.

Speak soon,

Amen.

Influencer Outreach E-mail For A Clothing Brand - Good Example

Subject used: Loved your last post about fashion

Hi Jessica, How are you?

I'm currently working with Immacul8 Clothing and wanted to see if you would be interested in collaborating with us.

We've been following you for a while and we loved your last post on fashion with that little black dress on [blog url].

We would be happy to send out any of the following products for you, for free - to feature as part of a blog post and maybe a couple of social media posts:

- Any of our new arrivals - http://immacul8collection.com/new-arrivals
- Any of our top sellers - http://immacul8collection.com/sale

Please let me know if there's any other products you like that are not on 'new arrivals' or 'top sellers' and i'll speak with the management team and see if we can still get them sent out for you :).

We'd like to ask for you to include at least 3 photos and link to [brand website] in the post. If this sounds like something you would like to go forward with, just let me know which clothing items you like most and the sizes you require!

We would also love to pay out commission on any sales generated from your post, we can track this by offering you a unique voucher code 'JESSICA10' which also entitles your followers to 10% off any of ours products.

You can find us on Instagram @immacul8collection.

Many Thanks

Amen.

What's great about this email is that we give all the necessary information up front. Putting your offer on the table and being clear about what you would like in return not only shows the blogger that you're honest and easy to work with, but it also gives the blogger time to weigh up their thoughts.

It's great because we've offered the influencer free products, we even mentioned that they can select products from the categories that aren't open to other influencers, offered the influencer commission on sales and offered a 10% voucher code for their followers to enjoy. It's a win-win situation, the only reason the influencer is likely to not reply is because 1) The subject wasn't good enough and the email wasn't opened. 2) The influencer is already tied with another brand offering the same products or services.

Bonus Tip

Download a piece of software that informs you if an email has been read or not (we recommend Sidekick by HubSpot). This helps you understand which 'subject' titles and email content have the best response rates. If ten of your e-mails have been read and you've had zero replies you need to work on the email pitch. If you've sent ten e-mails and had zero opens, then you'll need to tweak your subject title.

Follow Up

Contrary to some very wrong beliefs, most influencers are actually quite busy. Many influencers also tend to use separate email accounts than their personal ones (just like your company might), and so can forget to sign in and check for emails. If you haven't heard back, it is always worth sending a polite follow up emails to check that they received the original one, and ask if they'd had any thoughts about the opportunity of working with your brand.

Tweet or Instagram message them after 2 weeks - If you still haven't heard I have to admit, some influencers can be difficult to track down. High profile influencers are often so heavily bombarded with emails that they simply can't ever get around to replying to every e-mail. In this case, once a week has past since your second email, we would recommend sending them a Tweet or Instagram message to check if they've received anything, but nothing too intrusive.

Know when to give up - Revisit your pitch and do not pester. If you haven't heard anything even after all of the above, give up. Either they have received your messages and aren't able to work with you (and don't have time to reply), or you can assume that it probably won't be easy to communicate with them if you do work together, so you're better of leaving it.

When An Influencer Emails You

You'll notice that as your brand grows, influencer's will reach out to you with opportunities to collaborate. It's important for you to check whether working with influencers that reach out to you are worth your time and not just looking for a freebie.

It could be that you've received an email from a really high influencer, which can happen as some influencers hire assistance to mailshoot brands all day or it could be a new blogger hoping to bag themselves a deal and some freebies to build content for their website.

Take your time to read through the email in full, see what they want in exchange for the promotion of your brand and work out how valuable they could by checking the number followers, likes and comments they receive on an average post.

Social Media Marketing

Social media networks are fantastic resources for businesses of all sizes looking to promote their products and services online. The social platforms themselves are free to use, although they have paid advertising options specifically for brands wanting to reach out to a wider audience.

If you want to create a successful social media strategy, you need to familiarise yourself with how each network operates, the kinds of customers you can reach and how your business can best use each platform.

Why Your Business Should Be Using Social Media

Increase Trust And Confidence

With so many different companies to choose from online, customers are often overwhelmed and look for an easy way to authenticate a business that they are dealing with for the first time. If they see that your business is active on social, it helps to fill potential customers with trust and should anything go wrong, that it will be easy for them to contact you.

Deliver A Better Customer Service

Social media sites (mainly Twitter) are often a first port of call for many customers who have pre-sales or support related questions. Leaving customer questions unattended makes your business look unprofessional, so it's crucial that you are visible on social networks that your customers are using, and that you are regularly monitoring all of your channels for brand mentions and customer enquiries.

Build A Brand Identity

Social media makes it easy to improve brand awareness and build your brand's identity. You can effectively establish your brand's personality and give your business a voice (also known as 'look and feel') that people can relate to. Connecting on an emotional level or showing some personality are both effective ways of helping your brand stand out from your competitors.

Promote Your Content

We all know how important content marketing is, not only in terms of SEO, but in order to attract new customers. Help increase awareness of each new blog article or news post that you publish, by posting them on your social media channels. A highly effective way to attract new customers is by posting high quality content on your social channels.

Keep Your Customers Engaged

Social media is a great way of keeping your business or brand in the mind of your customers. By posting valuable content you can actively influence purchasing decisions and help to foster customer loyalty and encourage repeat purchases.

Which Social Media Platforms To Use

With a new social media platform opening every other month, it can be confusing to know which platforms you should be using for your business. We understand that you don't have infinite time and resources to be everything to everyone. You can't afford to be on every social media site, but you can't afford to ignore them either. It's important to choose the platforms that work for you, your business goals, and what your customer wants and needs.

The best way we found to identify which social media platforms you should be using for your business include;

Demographics

First you will need to understand who your target audience is and what demographics you want to reach out to and then using this data sign up to the social sites that match your demographics.

For example, if you run a fashion brand and your target audience is under 25s, then you will want to consider your main platforms to be Instagram, Snapchat and Twitter as the majority users of these platforms meet a similar demographic.

This is not saying that you can't open a different platform such as Facebook, but it can help indicate what is right for your industry.

The next best method is by checking to see what your competitors are using and to check how many people search for your products or services on each platform.

To check what social media platforms your competitors are using, simply visit their website and see which social media icons they advertise.

Once you've identified which social platforms they use, you will need to open each one to see how active they've been and how often they receive likes and comments. This works best when checking well established businesses within your industry, so if your competitors are fairly new, it's best to perform a Google search and check other competitors that are ranked highly.

The third method to check which platforms are best for your industry is by performing what we call a 'social volume search'. Visit each social platform and use their search feature to see how many people are talking about your products or services.

For example, let's say you run a Beauty Salon business in Manchester.

Head over to Instagram, and use their search feature by typing in keywords such as 'Beauty Salon' and 'Body Massage'. This will show you how many people have used or searched for these terms in the past. If the search volume is high, it's worth using the social platform, if its low - consider giving it a miss.

Repeat this task for other social channels with a search facility to see if your customers are using these social platforms to look for the products or services you offer.

Facebook

Facebook is still the biggest social network, both in terms of name recognition and the total number of users. With more than 1.6 billion active users, Facebook is a great social media platform for connecting to people from all over the world with your business.

Considering that Facebook has several options for growing business exposure, it's a great starting point for your business, regardless of your industry. You can use it to share photos, videos, important business updates and more.

Benefits of Using Facebook

- Having a Facebook business page will make your business discoverable. When people search for your business on Facebook, they'll be able to find you.

- Have one-to-one conversations with your customers, who can like your Page, read your posts and share them with friends, and check in when they visit.

- Your page can help you to reach large groups of people frequently, with messages tailored to their needs and interests.

- Facebook Insights (analytics) can give you a deeper understanding of your customers and your marketing activities.

- Not only can you reach more people through Facebook, you can reach the specific people who are most likely to become your customers.

Setting up a Business Like Page

Your Facebook campaign should start with a Like / Business page, not a friends page. If you don't have a Facebook Like page head over to www.facebook.com/pages/create. We don't want to bore you with the basics so we've quickly noted down the things you need to do to optimise your Facebook page;

- Upload a Facebook profile picture (180 x 180)
- Upload a Facebook cover - include a call to action within the cover image if possible (Loads fastest as an sRGB JPG file that's 851 pixels wide, 315 pixels tall and less than 100 kilobytes)
- Add a business bio / description
- Add your opening hours (if possible)
- Add a business address
- Add contact details
- Add a gallery

To help you find and connect with potential customers, you will need to consider:

- What do your ideal customers have in common?
- How old are they and where do they live?
- How can your business help them?
- Would one group be more interested in specific messages, products or services? A sale or a timely offer?

To build your audience and gain more Facebook Likes, encourage your current customers and supporters to like your Facebook Page.

How To Promote Your New Facebook Like Page

- Adding a 'Like' button / widget to your website.

- Promoting your Like Page on e-mails and flyers.
- Offering a discount to customers who Like your Facebook Page.
- Adding your Facebook Page URL to your receipt or invoices.
- Inviting your friends to grow your Likes.

Our top 5 tips of keeping your Facebook Like Page active;

Use A Recognisable Profile Picture

You'll want to use a profile picture that will be easy for your customers to recognise. This could be anything from your company logo or if you're an individual even a professional looking headshot of yourself. Having a recognisable profile picture is important to getting found and 'Liked', especially in Facebook Search. Your profile image is displayed at the top of your Facebook Page, and is also shown when your profile has been shared, liked or commented.

Add A Call To Action Button

It's worth adding a call to action to your Facebook cover, like the 'Shop Now' example below.

There is a range of call to actions you can select from. Below we summarise the best ones based on our experiences.

Book Now - Use this button if you offer consultations, appointments or restaurant bookings.

Shop Now - Like the example shown, it's great for companies selling products online.

Contact Us - If you're selling a service or products that aren't bought online, for example a new car from a dealership. You really want to make use of a contact us button, in order to have initial engagement with potential customers.

Sign Up - Grow your e-mail list and offer a discount to your customers for signing up.

We also see an increase in engagement when the cover image is changed every month.

Content & Formats

When posting content you'll want to mix and match the type of formats you use. A recent case study conducted by Facebook shows that videos and photo posts get more engagement than any other type of post. However you'll want to publish normal text based post from time to time to keep all of your followers happy.

Use The Pin Feature

When you post new content to your Facebook Page, older posts get pushed further down your timeline. However sometimes you'll have that one post that performances ten times better than any other post you've published. When this happens you'll want to 'pin' the post so it stays at the top of the page. It's also worth pinning anything you're trying to promote like an upcoming event or product/service announcement.

Monitor And Respond To Comments

There's nothing worse than an inactive Facebook Page. If you've took your time to set up a Facebook Like Page, make sure you're using it and replying to comments. While it may not be necessary to respond to every comment, you should definitely monitor the conversations (especially any criticism) and aim to respond as often as possible.

Facebook Analytics

With Page Insights, Facebook makes it easy for you to track how well your page is doing. Page Insights is accessible via the Insights button at the top of your Facebook page, but at least 30 people need to like your page before this feature becomes available to you.

Facebook Remarketing

If you don't run a remarketing campaign for your business, you're pretty crazy. Facebook Remarketing is a powerful way for you to reach people on Facebook after they've visited your website. This helps you re-engage with those who have already shown an interest, making your adverts even more impactful.

Generally, remarketing on Facebook helps boost conversions and lowers the overall cost per customer acquisition. However, the biggest advantage of Facebook remarketing is that you're only showing your advert to users who are genuinely interested in your product because they've visited your website in the past.

How Remarketing Works

You've probably experienced remarketing at some point during your time online. Let's run with Amazon as our example to explain exactly how it works.

You visit Amazon to buy a new TV, you're spoilt for choice as you look at several different ones that take your fancy. You then leave Amazon's website without purchasing to have a think about which one you're going to buy. You jump on to Facebook to see what your friends are up to and you see an Amazon advert in your news feed, advertising the TVs you were considering to buy.

You then either a) consider clicking the advert to go back to Amazon and do a little more research, b) purchase the TV or c) or ignore it.

If you click the advert to do a little more research and go back off Amazon without making a purchase, Amazon will remarket the TV banner ads again.

If you were to click and purchase, the remarketing will come to a stop. If you've seen the advert but didn't take any action, the advertiser (Amazon) doesn't get charged. The advert will continue to appear until you have either purchased the product or the cookie (code) expires on your device.

We've got so many amazing case studies for Facebook & Google remarketing, it's just so powerful that it works for every industry. If you want to see which brands/websites are currently using remarketing on you, then visit www.heartcms.com/freetools.

Here's a few tips for Facebook Remarketing;

Drive Conversions And Build Brand Awareness

We all know converting first-time visitors into buyers can be a difficult take. If your industry is competitive, people are likely to browse multiple websites before completing a purchase of your product or service. In most cases, people visit a website, and then click away so they can compare prices with other websites. When they've left your website, some visitors may forget your name and you end up losing a sale because they can't find their way back to your site, or maybe they missed that one selling point that could have made the difference and closed an instant purchase.

Remarketing to your website visitors who didn't convert (make a purchase or enquiry) works to remedy those situations. When those visitors see your ad on their Facebook news feed, your brand automatically becomes more recognisable and that increases your chances of completing the purchase cycle and closing a sale. You can remarket brand awareness banners, so website visitors see your brand/logo and a list of products or services. Alternatively, you can set your remarketing campaigns so the website visitors see banners for the exact same product or services they were looking at on your website.

Experiment With All Website Visitors

You can also set your remarketing campaigns to be seen by all your website visitors, regardless if they purchased a product/service or not. This is worth doing if your business supplies a product or service which can be re-purchased (online e-commerce store) or if your customers are likely to use your more than once (restaurant).

Experiment With Duration

When you create a Facebook remarketing campaign, the default duration will be set to 30 days. So you can reach anyone who visited specific pages of your website during the past 30 days. That's great and very valuable, however you have other options too. You can build a remarketing campaign with durations up to 180 days. So if you're in an industry where you know your customers browse before they buy (travel agent, e-commerce store etc) then always set your duration to 180 days.

Facebook And Instagram Ads

Some of you may already know that Facebook purchased Instagram back in 2012, so the reason for us linking Facebook and Instagram Ads together in this book - is because they both use Facebook Ads Platform (also known as Facebook Business Manager / Power Editor).

As we've already established Facebook (and Instagram) have an incredible reach. However, it's not the number of Facebook users that makes Facebook Ads a unique advertising platform. It's the opportunity to advertise to the exact people you want to, that makes Facebook so powerful.

Since Facebook request users to add their information on signup, including; Age, Gender, Relationship Status, Job Title etc - an advertiser such as yourself can be very specific when deciding who to show your Facebook Ads to.

In this Facebook / Instagram guide we will go through what you need to do to step up and manage a successful Ads campaign.

Facebook Ads are purchased on an auction basis, where you, the advertiser are charged based on either clicks, impressions or actions. There are many different ad formats offered by Facebook, so in this guide we will provide you with a structured view of what opportunities you have as a business using the Facebook Ads platform.

Different Types of Ad Formats

Currently (as of March 2016) Facebook has 12 different types of ad formats. Below we briefly explain each one and it's benefits.

Boost Your Posts - Also Available For Instagram

Boost format Ads are used regularly by Facebook and Instagram advertisers. Boosting a post is the easiest and quickest type of ad you can run on Facebook. To run a boost post, simply publish a normal post on your Facebook newsfeed and then click the blue 'boost post' button and set a target audience for your advert.

Promote Your Page

A great way to gain Likes to your Facebook Business page and gain more exposure for your Facebook page.

Send People To Your Website - Also Available For Instagram

We love using this ad format to advertise products or services on a website. We normally use this ad format to advertise for brand awareness, if you're trying to make sales then use 'increase conversions on your website'.

Increase Conversions on Your Website - Also Available For Instagram

The best ad format we found to increase sales using Facebook and Instagram Ads is by running this type of campaign. Facebook allow you to create a pixel (conversion tracking code) to add to your website's checkout/thank you page. This helps you understand how many conversions have come from your Facebook ads.

Installs of Your App - Also Available For Instagram

Very good if you have an app and you're trying to increase installs.

Special Offer Claims

We use this ad format everyday as it's great for providing limited offers.

Other Ad Formats

- Get video views
- Collect leads for your business
- Increase Brand Awareness
- Increase engagement in your app
- Reach people near your business
- Raise attendance at your event

If you would like to learn more about these ad formats please check out our blog posts.

What To Consider When Setting Your Ads Campaign

Define Your Unique Selling Points

Explain what is unique about your company. Why should people looking for your products or services choose you over your competitors. If your business has any awards or accreditations, use them in your adverts and posts.

Use Eye-Catching Images

The imagery will make or break an advert. It's what draws the eye, and without a great attention grabber, you will have a hard time attracting clicks. When you create and design ads for Facebook, make sure you put effort into choosing images. This will have a huge impact on the end result. In many cases it will be the deciding factor whether or not the ad becomes successful.

Choose An Attractive Heading

Look at your unique selling points and include them in the title, preferably with a clear call-to-action that makes people want to click through to purchase a product.

Include A Description

In the description you'll want to include a small snippet of the main offer/content you're providing that helps explain the image you've used.

Split Test

It's very important that when planning a Facebook campaign you duplicate it a couple of times and make changes to the image or headline. In doing so, you will get an answer of what works best – what type of ad gets most clicks and what ads generates most sales or likes. You can then start pausing the ads that don't do as well as the others.

Define Age Groups To Target

You should always test your ads to different age groups to see how people react to your ads.

Gender Targeting

Are your products/services aimed at both males and females? Use your own data combined with Facebook insights to see which gender engages with your Facebook posts and consider setting your ads to match this data.

Define Your Target Location

If you run a business that has a physical location, then the settings will be pretty straightforward to advertise towards people in your area. However if you run an online business of some kind, whereby people can sign up to from all over the world, then test where your Facebook campaign is most successful by split testing different locations.

Relationship Status

A great tool to target Facebook and Instagram users based on their relationship status. For example if you run a restaurant and want to target couples for valentines, well - there's no better way to do it! (checkout our Indian Restaurant - Valentines Facebook Ads case study on our website).

Advertising Budget

Before you start your Facebook advertising campaigns, make a plan of how much you're willing to spend per day. Take into consideration that you might have to spend some initial money on the testing phase, before you know what type of ads your audience responds to.

Facebook Quality Score

Similar to Google Adwords (discussed later), Facebook and Instagram Ads use 'relevance score' to determine how relevant and successful a campaign is to help ensure that people see ads that matter to them.

How Relevance Score Works

Relevance score is calculated based on the positive and negative feedback Facebook expect an ad to receive from its target audience. The more positive interactions expected, the higher the ad's relevance score will be. (Positive indicators vary depending on the ad's objective, but may include video views and conversions, etc.)

The more times Facebook expect people to hide or report an ad, the lower its score will be. Ads receive a relevance score between 1 and 10, with 10 being the highest. The score is updated as people interact and provide feedback on the ad campaign. Ads with guaranteed delivery — like those bought through reach and frequency — are not impacted by relevance score. Relevance score has a smaller impact on cost and delivery in brand awareness campaigns, since those ads are optimised for reaching people, rather than driving a specific action like app installs.

Why Relevance Score Matters

Understanding Facebook's relevance score can help your business spend less on Facebook.

It can lower the cost of reaching people. Put simply, the higher an ad's relevance score is, the less it will cost to be delivered. This is because Facebook's ad delivery system is designed to show the right content to the right people, and a high relevance score is seen by the system as a positive signal.

Of course, relevance isn't the only factor Facebook's ad delivery system considers. Bid matters too. For instance, if two ads are aimed at the same audience, there's no guarantee that the ad with an excellent relevance score and low bid will beat the ad with a good relevance score and high bid. However, overall, having strong relevance scores will help your campaigns see more efficient delivery through Facebook's advertising platform system.

How To Use Relevance Score For Better Ads

While understanding relevance scores has real benefits for your ad campaigns, it's important to keep this metric in perspective. Relevance scores should not be used as the primary indicator of an ad's performance. As has long been the case on Facebook, the most important factor for success is bidding based on the business goal you hope to meet with an ad.

Let's say for instance you own a Restaurant Takeaway business and want to run a campaign that drives people to order through your website. Achieving the desired outcome (in this case, driving sales online) is ultimately more important than your relevance score. If you have an average score (between 5-7) but your ad is working, you may not want to change anything. Alternatively you may consider tweaking the ad to see how you can get lower cost of delivery by improving the relevance score.

You might monitor your relevance score, along with the sales you're driving, to learn when it's time to update your campaign. Use relevance scores as a way to reach your audiences at lower cost, and to test and learn about your ad creative and ad targeting.

Tips To Improve Your Relevance Score

When your ads are displayed to Facebook users, users can respond negatively by clicking 'I don't want to see this ad', or respond positively by clicking 'share' or clicking the advert. The Relevance Score improves as more people respond positively to your advert. Relevance scores will are based between 1-10, (5-7 being average).

Split Testing

Images take up a major portion of Facebook ads and are usually the first thing noticed by users as they scroll through the News Feed. As a result, they have a significant impact on your conversion rate. That's why it is important to split test different images to find out what is working (and being liked and shared) and what doesn't work.

Be Specific

When creating a target audience for your campaign, try to be as specific as possible when defining interests, age, gender, etc. If you achieve a better score with precise targeting, slowly fine tune your campaign from there, or use the targeting list with a better Relevance Score to create dedicated campaigns for different audience segment, each with tailored copy and ads.

Improve Your Call To Action

Facebook's call to action buttons can include words that tempt audiences to take action, thereby improving your score. Conversion rates may improve when users clearly understand the object of the ad, and when it's relevant, they are likely to take action.

Use Videos

Facebook ads featuring videos perform much better than regular ads, or even ads with other visuals such as compelling images and info-graphics. So it makes sense to use videos as they should improve your Relevance Score. On Facebook, you can directly create video ads and use the new video views feature to show them to people who are likely to find them interesting and take action depending on the CTA of the video. You can also split-test video content. For instance, if you create a 2-minute video and people lose interest at the 1 minute mark, you may want to change content at that mark or even shorten your video.

Instagram

We love instagram and so should you. We honestly believe that any and every business can use Instagram to grow their business and their audience. We realise that Instagram may not be ideal for every business, however the choice to grow a presence on Instagram will depend on your business, your goals, and your audience and customers. Instagram lets you put visual content in front of your target audience without any silly character limitations. Instagram is becoming a very popular social media platform and being under the Mark Zuckerberg umbrella, it means it's only going to get bigger and better.

While there always seems to be some trendy new social media platform on the horizon that everyone is talking about, Instagram is way past that. Having reached over 150 million active users faster than any other social media platform (except Google+), it's easy to say that this site is a force to be reckoned with. With many of the world's top 100 brands using Instagram, it's not just where the "kids" hang out. With the growth that Instagram has experienced since it was launched in 2010, and grown even bigger since Facebook took over - it is quickly establishing itself as one of the "biggest" social media sites.

If you own a smartphone such as an iPhone then you automatically own a half decent camera and there should be no reason why you can't use your device to keep your Instagram feed as active as possible. By using Instagram, your company can shoot, edit and share photos that activity engages potential customers with your brand.

Instagram is a personal communication platform that allows your company to participate and visualise the image of your brand, or reflect the brand via its consumers. When potential customers follow you on Instagram, they receive access to the parts of the business that they wouldn't normally see (kind of backstage access). This can create both loyalty and a more personal relationship. Instagram can also help create traffic towards your channels such as YouTube subscribers, Facebook Likes and offer claims.

Benefits of Using Instagram

There are lots of perks that Instagram can generate for your business, so let's have a look at the top 5 benefits.

Increased Engagement

Having an active Instagram account with useful and interesting content can earn you high levels of engagement with your followers. A recent case study found that Instagram content generates 58 times more engagement per follower than Facebook.

Increase Website Traffic

Although you can't add clickable URLS to Instagram posts, you can add a link to your profiles bio. Plus with the higher levels of engagement than on Facebook and Twitter, creating and maintaining a strong profile could be hugely beneficial for your website's visibility.

Building Trust And Personality

With branded content being a popular source for generating engagement, one of the key benefits of Instagram is that it can help you build brand trust. People buy from people and Instagram will help you to create that emotional connection with your audience.

Your Instagram Marketing Strategy

Being successful on Instagram takes more than publishing attractive images, it is the product of thoughtful strategy, a well-defined brand identity grounded in visual creativity and effective community management.

Determine Your Objectives

Before starting your Instagram journey (or fixing your current one), you'll want to consider the following when creating your strategy for Instagram;

- What will Instagram allow your business to do that isn't possible on other social networks?

- Who is your target audience?

- How can you integrate Instagram to your website and other social media platforms?

Instagram's focus on photo sharing offers a unique platform to showcase your business and people in addition to your products and services. The nature of the app lends itself to quickly capturing moments, giving your followers a chance to interact with your brand in a way that can feel more casual and instantaneous than on other networks such as Twitter or Facebook. Depending on your industry and KPI's, your Instagram strategy might target several of the following objectives:

- Increase brand awareness
- Advertise and promote your products or services
- Recruit new talent
- Grow your community
- Connect with influencers
- Share news
- Promote events

Build A Content Strategy

Content is the foundation to any social network site, and knowing when and what to post can make or break your campaigns.

The right approach for Instagram is one that best showcases your brand. Based on your target audience and objectives you will need to plan to deliver eye-catching content on a consistent basis.

Build A Look And Feel

Instagram is purely based on visual content (images and videos), so it's important to get the right look and feel to showcase your brand. Your images/video need to be thumb stoppers when your customers are scrolling down their feed.

For other channels, you would write up your content and then schedule them, then get your assets for the copy. However, for Instagram it's more important to get your assets first, and then come up with the content.

(Why not give us a follow - @HeartCMSUK)

If you're a brand that provides products, you'll want to showcase them visually. However, don't have product after product after product. Try adding motivational and inspirational quotes, behind the scenes footage, notes, tips and hints that can be engaging for your fans.

If you provide a service, you might consider it to be difficult for you to visually showcase your business. However, you should take this opportunity to advertise your services as a portfolio or an educational platform for your followers. Take a look at our Instagram for an example of this;

As you can see the top three posts promote news about the latest trends in the world of technology. Whereas the three images in the middle advertise a portfolio of a recent website and app that we have developed for our customers.

Once you've come up with content ideas, you'll want to mix it up so your not posting too much of the same thing over and over again.

The idea is to understand what your audience want to see and then build a database of content to post and schedule in your content calendar.

Set A Content Calendar

To establish a follower base on Instagram, you will need to determine the frequency of when and how often you post. To do this, we recommend that you develop a content calendar that cycles through your look and feel.

To determine your best posting times, you will need to trial and error your posting times until you have enough data to understand when your followers are online and engaging with your post.

Instagram Tips

Here's a few tips to make sure your Instagram pages attracts the correct audience and brings traffic and conversions to your website.

Link Up

For some reason many companies forget or don't know how to integrate Instagram to other social media channels. By connecting as many social media channels to your Instagram means you only need to update and publish images using your Instagram account and all your social channels will update.

To connect your Instagram to other social sites, head over to options/settings and then click Linked Accounts.

Use Less Text

This should be clear by now, but the more your ad looks like a native post, the more likely you're going to see an above-average return on your investment. Instagram's all about visuals, think of Instagram as the social network for art.

If you take a look at the 10 most popular trending photos as you're reading this, you'll see that hardly any photos contain text.

Engage With Your Followers

If a new fan likes what you're posting and hits the follow button, be sure to head over to their Instagram profile and make them feel apart of your community.

When writing your copy remember that with Instagram's latest update you have a restricted amount of characters before it then provides a 'see more' button. You roughly have 140 visible characters, before the see more button appears. So it is important to get your unique selling point across in the first few characters.

Hashtags

While hashtags originated on Twitter, they quickly became apart of each social media as a whole. Instagram hashtag density tends to be much greater than Twitter's because companies realise the success of their Instagram marketing depends on using high valuable hashtags.

One of the most powerful methods Instagram users use to source content is to search with hashtags. Consider hashtags the keywords of Instagram, for example, a seo agency might post a picture of a day in the office at Google HQ in London, and then use the hashtags #seo #agency #google and #london when uploading to Instagram.

By using these hashtags, the image is saved so other Instagram users who search for images related to #SEO can find it.

Twitter

Still known as one of the most used social media platforms within the business world, the short message communication tool allows you to send and receive tweets of up to 140 characters long.

The significant push towards both social media and branding has made it nearly impossible to avoid using Twitter for your business. Whether you're educating customers about your product or service, reaching a new audience or promoting your brand, Twitter is one of the most useful places to be to achieve your marketing goals.

Setting Up A Twitter Account

To ensure you get off to the good start, here are some easy-to-follow tips on how to optimise a Twitter account for your business.

Choosing Your Twitter Username

Nothing expresses your brand on Twitter more than your profile username. This name appears next to all of your tweets, and is how people identify you on Twitter. When deciding a name for your Twitter account, avoid using punctuations to keep your name easy to type on mobile devices. If your exact business name is not already to use, then choose a similar name for consistency.

Profile Images

Twitter has two different types of images that will represent your business. It's important that you take advantage of using both image sets and upload eye catching images. Your main profile picture is a typical square photo that appears next to all the tweets you send out. Similar to our suggestions for Facebook, you can either use your company logo or a personal headshot.

Build A Strong Profile

It's very important that you complete your Twitter profile settings to help gain maximum exposure. In the profile settings tab you will find the following:

Location Settings

This feature enables you to tell people where they can find you, great for local businesses to advertise their physical location.

Website Details

You'll want to share your web address with your followers.

Bio

You get up to 160 characters to tell people what your business is about and what you have to offer. Skip your mission statement and talk about the benefits your products or services deliver. Make it short and snappy but clear and precise.

Twitter Tips

Join In

It's not just about what you can provide and what you would like to talk about when it comes to Twitter. It's worth having a look at what your community/fans are talking about. You can do this by using the search feature on Twitter or even by looking on popular blog sites for related news.

Once you have something to talk about, join in the conversation and try to help others online.

For example, if you are a fashion brand and you see #Oscars trending, you can join in the conversation as a fashion expert and talk about the eye-popping moments as celebrities walk the red carpet.

Another example could be if you run a dentist business and you see #NationalSmileDay trending on the popular page. You should take full advantage and join the conversation.

Growing Your Twitter Followers

For those of you who already have a Twitter account let's share some useful tips on increasing your Twitter followers.

Unless you're a celebrity like Justin Bieber or Kim Kardashian, you're going to have to work hard on building your initial following on Twitter. To do this, you'll want to see a month or two to make Twitter you're primarily social media account and double up on your posts and tweets.

Analytical data shows that the more you Tweet, the more followers you're likely to gain. If you're Twitter account is fairly new or hasn't been very active, this is probably the best time to dedicate yourself to Twitter. Your initial immersion will pay off in terms of "market research," as well: you'll sharpen your brand's voice, get comfortable with the medium and its quirks such as hashtags, @ replies, and learn the types of content that appeal to and engage your followers.

Use timesaving tools and schedule your Tweets - There's lots of free tools that you can use to schedule your Tweets. This is a fantastic way to spend a weekend to set up the following week's content for Twitter and set times that best engage with your followers. You can find a list of free Twitter tools at www.heartcms.com/freetools.

Respond to users who are interested in similar content - When you comment, retweet or even favorite a Tweet, other Twitter users will notice that your share a similar interest in content and therefore will be inclined to follow you.

Retweet inspirational quotes - Regardless of your industry, posting inspirational quotes is one of the very few methods that will guarantee you likes. Quotes tend to see higher engagement on Twitter because people enjoy reading them and retweeting them. Remember to always hashtag your #quotes.

Twitter's Algorithm

Your customers will follow hundreds of people on Twitter, maybe thousands, so when they open Twitter your content can be easily missed. It is therefore important to know the best timings to post by split testing and reviewing your data through analytics. With Twitter's recent updates they have shared a new timeline feature that helps their followers to catch up on the best Tweets based on people they follow, as well as past interests.

How It Works

When you open Twitter after being away for a while, the tweets you're most likely to care about will appear at the top of your timeline, still recent and in reverse chronological order. The rest of the tweets will be displayed right underneath, also in reverse chronological order, as always.

We've already seen that people who use this new feature tend to Retweet and Tweet more, creating more live commentary and con-versations, which is great for everyone, especially for you as a business. If you provide your customers engaging fun content, they are not only likely to keep following you but also see your content at the top of their new feeds.

Twitter Ads

It's important to say that Twitter's Ad platform is relatively basic if directly compared to Facebook and Instagram's Ad network. Unfortunately you'll find that the target settings for Twitters ads are very broad and this is largely due to Twitter requesting less information on signup than Facebook, but that's not to say the platform can't be successful.

There are three different types of ad formats on Twitter:

Promote account - This ad format suggest accounts that people don't currently follow and may find interesting. Promoted accounts can help boost your follower growth, they are best used when you would like to be more discoverable to people who are likely to love your business.

Consistently growing your follower base on Twitter will help you achieve the following goals:

- Drive purchases, leads, downloads, and signups - By choosing to follow you, Twitter users are demonstrating an interest in your product. You have an opportunity to connect with them in meaningful ways to drive actions.

- Increase brand awareness and word of mouth sharing - When you Tweet valuable content, Twitter makes it easy for your followers to share it with their friends through retweets, driving increase reach and awareness.

- Drive web traffic - Once you acquire a paid follower you have the opportunity to engage with them everyday, for free, with your organic Tweets. Your followers are the mostly like to see your Tweets and spend time on your website.

Promoted Tweets - Are regular Tweets with the added bonus that they can reach more people who are interested in your business. They should be used to place your best content in front of the audience that matters to you at the right time. If your goal is to drive a particular action via Twitter, Promoted Tweets are a great place to promote engaging content that includes a call to action to users.

Using Promoted Tweets you can:

- Drive website traffic by asking users to click on your best content

- Offer coupons and deals in the copy of your Tweets

- Drive leads using Lead Generation Cards

- Promote sales and giveaways

If your goal is to drive awareness for your business, Promoted Tweets can do this in a variety of ways:

- Expand the reach of your content like blog posts, white papers, and more

- Connect with influencers and brand advocates by ensuring they see your content

- Promote awareness around events and product launches

- Ask for retweets to gain an even broader audience for your messages

Promoted Trends - Are an extension of our Promoted Tweets platform, and are now a full-fledged product in their own right. With Promoted Trends, users see time-, context-, and event-sensitive trends promoted by Twitter's advertising partners. These paid Promoted Trends appear at the top of the Trending Topics list on Twitter and are clearly marked as "Promoted."

Users interact with Promoted Trends the same way they interact with any other Trending Topic. They are able to click on a Promoted Trend to view all Tweets containing the trending #hashtag or trend terms. They are also able to Tweet about the Promoted Trend by including the terms in their Tweets. The only real difference is that a Promoted Trend is purchased by an advertiser and clearly marked as being promoted.

Targeting your target customer on Twitter can be done in the following ways:

Gender - As it says on the tin, you can target both or each individual gender.

Location - You can choose the target location that you want your Tweets to be appear in. Note that if you target a specific postal code, your Tweets will show to people currently in that code, not necessarily those that live in that code. This is perfect for local stores that want to appear on the radars of people visiting the area, and the limited reach keeps costs relatively low.

Keywords - You can target Twitter users that have searched your target keywords, tweeted about them or engaged with them.

Interest Targeting - Target Twitter followers by category such as Automotive, Investments, Beauty etc.

LinkedIn

L inkedIn is by far one of the most underrated social media plat-forms for individuals and companies that are looking to make new connections, generate leads and build their brand. While it's an important platform for all businesses, LinkedIn can be a true game changer for B2B companies.

According to reliable sources LinkedIn has now surpassed Facebook as the number #1 most important social media site for B2B market-ers, and is the business-oriented social network of choice for most professionals.

LinkedIn Benefits

Although many people view the social media site LinkedIn only as a site for job hunters and for growing your professional network, Linke-dIn is an equally effective tool for generating new business leads and nurturing referral relationships.

Here's a few reasons why your business should be on LinkedIn.

Creating Shareable Content That Benefits Your Audience

By producing valuable content that users in your industry will want to see and share, helps you expand your global reach and influence. Make your content available in different formats such as blog posts, infographics, webinars and videos to suit the viewing preferences of your target audience.

Be Different And Establish Credibility

You'll find that not many of your competitors are yet on LinkedIn, take full advantage of this and show your customers that your brand is ahead of the game.

A LinkedIn profile give you the ability to interact with LinkedIn members in other areas of the site including groups and the answers section. In both groups and answers, you have the opportunity to demonstrate your company's expertise by participating in discussions related to your industry and answering questions from other LinkedIn members. By doing show, you'll be growing your brand's reach and credibility.

Other Social Media Platforms

Google Plus

Everyone's heard of Google Plus (Google +), but it seems like no-one is using it.

If you run a small to medium size business, here are some important reasons to why you should open and be active on your Google Plus account.

There are 111 million active accounts on Google Plus which is far less than other platforms. It's certainly not a slow market that you should ignore, in fact more opportunities are available for you to be visible to the active users who are using it.

If you want to sell your services or products then you would be crazy not to take the opportunity in posting on Google Plus. Why? Because even though people might not use it, the truth is Google love it! If we told you Google Plus can help your company rank higher in their search results, why wouldn't you use it?

When you post on Google Plus for Business Page it is immediately indexed by Google. Therefore your content can rank in search results even if your website doesn't which is a huge opportunity for your business.

Snapchat

You may be asking yourself, how could Snapchat possibly help my business, or you may already be thinking about using it.

When it comes to Snapchat, demographics is an important factor to knowing is Snapchat is suitable for your business.

The majority of Snapchat users are a much younger age group than the likes of Facebook and Twitter. So you need to ask yourself - does Snapchat have a place in my marketing strategy?

Snapchats user base is growing each day and will keep growing, with 100 million daily active users worldwide since 2014.

To give you an understanding of what their current demographic stats look like, we've included the most recent stats we could get hold of;

- **Age 18-24: 45%**
- **Age 25-34: 26%**
- **Age 35-44: 13%**
- **Age 45-54: 10%**
- **Age 55-64: 6%**

As you can see, the majority of Snapchat users are under 34. In reality, the age of Snapchat users may skew even lower as the numbers above does not include 13 – 17 year olds. From experience and talking to our customers, Snapchat will play a major role in reaching out to the younger generation.

Snapchat allows users to send and receive 'self-destructing' photos and videos which are called 'Snaps'. Unlike other platforms your posts (or snaps) don't stick around for very long.

In fact if you send a snap to a friend or follower on your list, it disappears once they have viewed it. However, if you post on your story then it can last up to 24 hours.

Here are some tips on how to use Snapchat;

Behind The Scenes

Give your fans a look at how your products are created or even a sneak peek of upcoming events. For example, if you are involved with London Fashion Week, take a few quick snaps on what is happening behind the curtain, or if you are at the factory where products are being made, grab a snap of the production process.

Whether you are a small business or a large corporate brand, the people who make your business run are important to you, so why not showcase this and give them credit for the work they do. Not only this, but your followers will feel like they know your brand and the people involved, which will increase the chances of them using your business.

Quick Tips And Advice

No-one knows your business the way you do, and you know why you are better than your competitors. Showcase your expertise with quick tips and advice that can demonstrate this. For example: If you run a restaurant business, you could do a quick snap on how to cut onions without the tears.

Snap It First

Give your followers a reason to keep coming back to your snaps. If you have new products being launched soon have a snap first on Snapchat before anywhere else where only your friends (i.e. followers) get to see before its official launch.

Giveaways

Reward your followers with competitions or special offers and discount codes!

Your Story

Share a slice of your life and show your followers what is happening day-to-day in your business. For example one of our clients 'Yiannimize' a vehicle wrapping company based in London, 'snap' about the cars they are working on. Most of the cars worked on are for celebrities so they'll make a quick snap with John Terry or the boys from One Direction and give their Snapchat audience something to talk about.

Given that the demographic is so young, the content you post needs to be fun and in some ways irrelevant. It's time to think outside the box and create content that will attract followers for your business.

Pinterest

Pinterest is a virtual pinboard where it allows you to organise and share creative images and content you upload or find on the web.

You can browse boards created by other people to discover new things and get inspiration from people who share your interests.

There are currently 2.5 Billion page views per month on Pinterest with over 100 million active users.

Pinterest helps people find creative ideas, that's why so many businesses, especially retailers have focused more of their marketing efforts on this platform.

Here are some benefits on how Pinterest can help your business;

Sizable Platform

With more than 100 million Pinners, Pinterest can help you reach your target audience when it comes to a creative and engaging brand.

Investing Time

Although you might think you don't have time, remember that pins last forever - your content doesn't have an expiry date.

Pinners Are Open To Brands

Unlike other channels, Pinners are opened to see what brands have to offer and don't mind seeing a bunch of content from the brand on their news feed as long as it is creative.

Influence Purchases

Pinners are engaged and love advocates to the channel. Pinners look for inspiration when it comes to Pinterest and save these images for when they next go shopping.

Pinners have larger shopping carts so it's something you want to think about when it comes to connecting your business to the board.

Trends

Pinterest informs you of upcoming and emerging trends and popular products. You want to think about this if you are in the fashion, beauty, home or garden industry. Pinterest display popular keywords and trending products in real time. When you use Promoted Pins, you can also track which products are in style or might be losing traction in the market. This info can help your business improve its line of products and services.

Google Adwords

So you've got a great product or service that you want to push and sell online. Your on-site SEO has been completed, you're working on your off-site SEO on a monthly basis and now you're ready to introduce Google Adwords to the mix.

Now, you're probably thinking do I really need Google Adwords for my business. The answer is simple. If you've gotten this far in the book it's because you want your business to be found online, and most importantly on Google.

While you might have done your SEO tasks and you're waiting for your rankings to increase based on the off-site SEO tasks you're doing. Google Adwords gives you the possibility of being found on page one of Google instantly.

Why Adwords

Google Adwords is an online advertising platform that sends potential customers searching for your products or services on Google straight to your website. It allows you (the advertiser) to appear and reach out to your target audience at the very moment that they're searching on Google for the things you offer. Plus, you only pay when they click to visit your website.

Measurable, Accountable, Flexible

Google AdWords shows how many people notice your ads and what percentage click to visit your website (known as Click Through Rate), or call you. With these tracking tools, you can even see the actual sales your website is generating as a direct result of your ads.

You can tweak your ads, try new search terms, pause your campaign and re-start whenever you like, all within the Google AdWords control panel.

In today's mobile world, you need to be advertising on every device that your customers are using – desktop, laptop, tablet and mobile. That way, when they're searching, browsing or buying, your ad will display.

How It Works

For those of you who have never used Google Adwords, we give you a quick simple guide on how it works.

Start by writing an ad that tells people what products or services you offer, then choose the search terms (keywords) that will make your ad show in the Google results. Finally, set a daily budget and your adverts go live.

If the search term people type in Google match your keywords, your advert will appear on Google as a sponsored listing.

Customers then click your ad and go to your website or call you directly. Best of all, you only pay if they click to your website or call your business.

Quality Score

Google as you know is all about numbers and rankings. Every campaign you set out is measured and assigned a place in Google's every day changing algorithms.

The Quality Score between 1-10 reported for each keyword in your account is an estimate of the quality of your ads and landing pages triggered by that keyword. Having a high Quality Score means that Google thinks that your ad and landing page are relevant and useful to someone looking at your ad.

Let's say that you own a website that sells mobile phones, and your potential customer is looking for a 'new iPhone 6s Plus'. Wouldn't it be great if your customer typed 'new iPhone 6s Plus' into Google search and saw your new offer about this device. They have then clicked your ad, landed on your web page and bought themselves a brand new iPhone 6s Plus. In this case, the customer searches and finds exactly what they were looking for. That's what Google consider a great user experience, and that's what can earn your keyword a high Quality Score.

Where on the other hand, your potential customer searches for a 'new iPhone 6s Plus' on Google and sees your advert about iPhones. They have clicked the ad and are presented with a landing page full of smartphones including iPhones and Android devices. This would receive a low Quality Score as the ad sent the customer to a landing page full of other devices and not exactly what the customer was looking for.

Results

Between our experienced team at HeartCMS we've managed over thousands of Pay Per Click campaigns and we've seen some phenomenal results.

We find that a lot of business owners are a little skeptical of using Google Adwords. The reason for this is because of the lack of understanding behind Adwords and not getting to grips with all the features that make or break a campaign.

Throughout this chapter, we explain how to setup a successful Google Adwords campaign and monitor conversions.

A Free Gift

As Google Partners we're able to offer two fantastic offers.

If you currently have a Google Adwords campaign running, we are able to offer a free Adwords review and consultation on your campaign and explain how it can be improved. To request a free review, head over to www.heartcms.com/adwordsoffer.

If your business is all new to Google Adwords, we're able to offer up-to £225* free advertising credit for your first 30 days. To see if your business is applicable for this offer, head over to www.heartcms.com/adwordsoffer.

*Offer subject to change

Do Your Research

Launching a new AdWords search campaign is an exhilarating process. If you're just starting your journey, then fear may be dominating your thoughts, so in this section of the book our goal is to explain everything you need to know, to make sure your campaign brings a ROI (return on investment).

The steps we're about to go through will ensure you're depositing more money into your business bank account, rather than just funding Google's empire.

Search Volume

If your customers are not searching for your products or services on Google, then Adwords may not be for your business. Before you get too excited about creating your first master campaign, we need to verify there is a high search volume for the products or services you offer.

The Google Keyword Tool which can be found at www.heartcms.com/freetools acts much like a thesaurus. You enter in keywords you think your customers are searching, and Google tells you other similar, relevant keywords. Google will also tell you how often people search these keywords, how competitive they are, and how much it'll cost to advertise each keyword.

All of this information will help you determine which keywords you want to use in your campaign.

Here's an example of some results when searching for keyword data on 'personal trainer';

Your product or service

personal trainer			Get id

Ad group ideas	Keyword ideas			Columns ▾	⬚	⬇ Downlc

Keyword (by relevance)	Avg. monthly searches ?	Competition ?	Suggested bid ?
personal training	⬚ 27,100	Medium	£2.15
fitness	⬚ 823,000	Low	£0.51
fitness trainer	⬚ 12,100	Medium	£1.44

As you can see the average search volume for these keywords are very high and worth targeting with Google Adwords. It also shows the suggested bid value for each keyword.

Now you might be thinking, £2.15 for a click for personal training? That's exactly how you should be thinking. If you consider the cost of the click and the potential return, you'll be able to workout an approximate cost per conversion. So for example, If the average 'personal training' click costs £2.15 and your cheapest personal training plan is £30, that's a cost per conversion of £27.85. Now what you have to remember is that not every click will convert, in fact your conversion rate can be anything from 1% to 50% and it will be impossible to know what your conversion rate is without running a campaign. As long as your product or service cost is more than the cost of advertising on Google, then it's worth adding as a keyword.

However if your product or service has a high basket/order value then the cost of the click should not be a concern. For example, if you sell household LED bulbs for £1.25, but you know that the average order value happens to be £12.50 (buying 10 bulbs at a time). Then the cost of advertising for the keyword 'LED bulbs' at £2.20 is not a concern because you know the likely chance of a customer buying a single bulb is going to be very rare.

Now using the Google Keyword Tool, you'll want to make a list of keywords that have a high search volume, low competition level and a cheap cost per click.

If you downloaded our spreadsheet, click onto the 'Adwords Search Volume' tab or make a spreadsheet similar to this;

	Keyword	Search Volume	Competition Level	Cost Per Click	RRP	Profit
Keyword						

Start filling your spreadsheet with all the data you find on the keywords for your products or services.

Updated example;

	Keyword	Search Volume	Competition Level	Cost Per Click	RRP	Profit
Keyword	Personal trainer nottingham	480	high	£1.25	£30	£28.75

Once you've built a list, you should have a clear idea of which keywords (products or services) are worth investing into for Google Adwords.

Competitor Lookout

At this point, you now have a list of "buying intent" keywords that you're confident your business can afford. The next step is to reduce your risk by leveraging competitor intelligence. In most industries, you'll find competitors who already have tested and optimised their AdWords campaigns. That means they have figured out which keywords, ads, and landing pages work well and produce a profitable return on investment.

Wouldn't it be great if you could just ask your competitor's to see their AdWords accounts and check over their successful campaigns? Well, we all know that's not going to happen. So let us introduce you to a very powerful competitive intelligence tool called KeywordSpy.

KeywordSpy collects, organises, and provides easy access to all of your competitors' historical advertising information. Though KeywordSpy does cost, they do offer a 14 day free trial. We recommend you go ahead and signup to your free trial and get as much research done on your competitors so you know what keywords they are targeting.

Come Up With A USP

Your USP (unique selling point), is what differentiates your business from your competitors and gives your potential customer a compelling reason to choose you. In other words, your USP answers the question "Why should I, your potential customer, choose to do business with you, over your competitors". Your USP should be advertised in your Google Ads and Landing Pages.

When it comes to Google AdWords, there are 3 important reasons to create a powerful USP.

First, a strong USP will generate more traffic from qualified prospects (encourage clicks to your ads) and repel unwanted leads (prevent wasted clicks to your ads).

Secondly, a strong USP will skyrocket your sales conversion rates. So, not only will you generate more traffic because you'll get more clicks to your ads, you'll also convert more of your traffic into paying customers.

Finally, a strong USP can eliminate price comparison shoppers. This can be a game changer for your business because you're no longer seen as a commodity. If you give your potential customers a compelling reason to do business with you against your competition, then price becomes a secondary issue, and you'll be able to demand higher prices than your competitors without affecting your conversion rates.

Some of you may already have a USP, therefore you will want to advertise these.

Such as;

- Award Winning
- Accredited Installers
- Free Next Day Delivery
- 30 Day Money Back Guarantee
- Best Selling
- As Featured on

For those of you who have just setup or want a stronger USP, here's a powerful USP I'm sure you'll recognise: "Fresh hot pizza delivered in 30 minutes or less, guaranteed."

That's Domino's Pizza's USP, and they used it to build a billion dollar empire. They don't claim to be all things to everybody. In fact, they don't even mention quality ingredients, price, or taste. They focused their entire business on the one thing their customers care about most – fast, on-time delivery. This is what makes a killer USP.

Exclusive Offers

What can you offer to your customers that is so compelling and believable that your potential customer would be a fool to not take action?

Your product or service must be more valuable than the price. That's basic marketing. This doesn't mean your offer has to be cheap. You just need to clearly define all of the value your product or service provides to your customer and make sure it outweighs your price tag.

When you make an offer that appears to be too good to be true, then your potential customer may be a little skeptical. So you must provide a believable reason for your offer.

For example, if you're running an exclusive sale for your e-commerce business that sells 'alarm systems', you'll need to give a reason why you're offering such a steep discount. The reason could be anything: clearing out inventory, end-of-the-year sale, celebrating the business anniversary, opening a new store, and so on.

Everyone is scared of getting ripped off online. One of the best tactics to minimise the risk to your customer is with a money back guarantee. A money back guarantee puts all the risk on your business to deliver excellent service, or else you'll have to give all the money back to the customer.

Whenever possible, we always recommend you include some kind of guarantee in your offer. It will improve your CTR (click through rate) and it's another great way to differentiate yourself from your competitors.

Setting Up Your Campaign

Now that you have a list of profitable keywords it's time to set up your campaign. If you don't have an Adwords account head over to www. google.co.uk/adwords. Contact us beforehand if you would like to get up-to £225* free advertising credit.

With Google AdWords, you pay only when people click on your ads. Therefore, your ads have three very important jobs:

- Attract qualified leads so they click your ad.
- Repel unqualified prospects so they don't eat into your budget.
- Improve Quality Score

Creating ads with a high click-through rate (CTR) will increase your AdWords Quality Score, which in turn will lower the cost per click of your keywords. So your ads will directly affect how much you pay per click for each of your keywords.

There are 7 key components to your AdWords text ads:

Headline
Description line 1
Description line 2
Display URL
Landing Page URL
Reviews
Site Extensions

Headline

The headline is the most important component because it's the first thing your potential customer will read. Try to include your keyword and location (if local business) in the headline of your ads, as Google will highlight keywords in bold, which makes it stand out from other ads.

Another great strategy we find that works is to ask a question in the headline. For example, if the keyword you've added is "bmw garage derby" then a compelling headline would be "Looking For a BMW in Derby?" Not only is part of the keyword in the headline, but the question will encourage the potential customer nodding their head to click the advert. AdWords allows up to 25 characters for your headline so make every letter count and use abbreviations whenever possible.

Description Lines

The two Description lines are limited to 35 characters each. In the first Description you will want to promote your product or service along with the offer. For the second Description line you'll want to mention your unique selling point.

Display URL

The display URL is an easily overlooked area of your ads. Don't just copy and paste your domain name. Instead, use your Display URL to include your offer, your call to action, your unique selling point, or anything else that will make your ads stand out.

Landing Page

Don't make the mistake made by a lot of first-time advertisers. Don't send your customers to your homepage. Instead, create a dedicated landing page that matches the keyword and the ad. The goal is to make the entire sales process as easy as possible so your potential customer is continually reassured they're going down the right path.

The most important component on your landing page is your headline, which is the first thing your potential customer will pay attention to. Your headline must grab attention, reiterate the offer made in the ad, and compel your potential customer to keep reading the rest of the page.

The content of your landing page should also be relevant to the keyword searched and the ad clicked on. Include your unique selling point, the benefits of your product or service, details about your irresistible offer, social proof, credibility that you're a legitimate business, and a strong call to action.

Reviews

When a customer comes to use you for the first time, they'll want reassurance that they are dealing with a legitimate company. You can and should introduce a review system, such as Google reviews to your ads.

When customers are searching for products or services online, there's nothing better than getting them to see a good review. With review extensions, you can share those positive write-ups, awards or third-party rankings with potential customers with an additional line of text beneath your ads on Google Search. You know your business is great, but review extensions let customers know that a respected third-party source agrees. Adding a quote from a positive review, award or accolade to the text beneath your ads gives potential customers one more reason to click.

Ad Extensions

Ad extensions are a type of ad format that show extra information ("extending" from your text ads) about your business. Some can be added manually and others are automated.

Ad extensions tend to improve your ad's visibility. They often appear above the search results, rather than along the sidebar. If two competing ads have the same bid and quality, then the ad with greater expected impact from extensions will generally appear in a higher ad position than the other.

Extensions can also help improve the click-through rate (CTR) of your ads. More clicks mean more customer traffic.

AdWords shows one or more extensions with your ad when it calculates that the extension (or combination of extensions) will improve your campaign performance. Let's have a look at the different types of extensions available.

App Extensions

App extensions showcase your mobile or tablet app by showing a link to your app below your ad. Clicking on this link can either lead to your app's description in the app store (Google Play or the Apple App Store), or simply begin downloading. Clicking on your ad's headline will still lead to your website.

Call Extensions

Encourage calls to your business by displaying your phone number on your ad. Show a clickable call button in your ad (on smartphones only). Cost for a call are the same as a headline click. For call-only campaigns, ads will only appear on devices capable of making calls.

Location Extensions

Location extensions show your business address, phone number and a map marker with your ad text. On mobile, they include a link with directions to your business. Clicks on ads with location extensions cost a standard cost per click.

Sitelink Extensions

The sitelinks ad extension shows links to specific pages on your website beneath the text of your ads (and in addition to the main landing page), helping customers to reach what they're looking for on your site with just one click. Sitelinks appear in the ads at the top and bottom of Google search results. You can add sitelinks when you create your campaign. You can edit your link text and URLs and see how ads that contain sitelinks perform, in the Ad extensions tab.

Callout Extensions

The callout ad extension lets you include additional text with your search ads. This lets you provide detailed information about your business, including the products and services that you offer. Callouts appear in ads at the top and bottom of Google search results. You can add callouts when you create your campaign. You can edit your descriptive text, and see how ads that contain callouts perform in the Ad extensions tab.

Ad Breakdown

Sometimes even big commercial companies get pay per click marketing wrong, so we're going to show you a live example;

Search term ' iPhone 6s plus'

Ad result from o2;

iPhone 6s Plus on O2 - o2.co.uk
Ad www.o2.co.uk/iPhone_6s_Plus ▾
3.7 ★★★★★ rating for o2.co.uk
Get **iPhone 6s Plus** Today. £9.99 Upfront On A £69 Tariff
Free tech support 24/7 · Superfast 4G Network · Coverage Across Country
♥ 67 High Road, Beeston, Nottinghamshire - 0115 922 2242

Let's break it down.

Headline = iPhone 6s Plus on O2 - o2.co.uk
Description 1 = Get iPhone 6s Plus Today. £9.99 Upfront On A £69 Traffic

Description 2 = Free tech support 24/7 - Superfast 4G Network - Coverage Across Country
Display URL = www.o2.co.uk/iPhone_6s_Plus
Landing Page = https://www.o2.co.uk/shop/phones/apple/iphone-6s-plus/
Reviews = 3.7 Google ratings
Site Extensions = Address and contact number.

The great thing about this advert from o2 is that the Ad content is clearly related to the search term and if a customer is to click the link, it's likely going to take them to a page where they can purchase an iPhone 6s plus.

We can see that the Headline is very related and the first line of Description also includes the keyword and has been highlighted by Google. O2 has also made it clear that this phone is on o2 so it's clear that this offer is for anyone on o2 or wanting to move to o2. Ideally this advert will repel customers on other networks such as EE looking for an upgrade within the same network (this should help reduce spend on wasted clicks).

In the second Description line o2 have included some great call to actions and unique selling points such as 'free tech support 24/7' and 'superfast 4G network'.

The Display URL has been optimised well and Google have put the keyword that is displayed in the URL as bold, to help the ad get more clicks.

One thing we did notice that o2 haven't done, is set a redirect on the display URL. The URL shown in this section is 'www.o2.co.uk/iPhone_6s_Plus' and is actually a made up destination and does't actually exist.

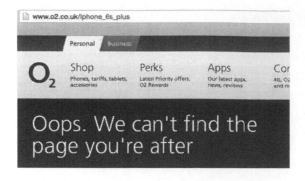

This is fine to do, and Google encourage you to do so to make the ad more relevant. However, we always recommend that you redirect these URLS just in case customers copy and paste or share these links.

The landing page itself is very relevant and directs the user to purchase a new iphone 6s plus which will help the keywords overall Quality Score.

The advert also integrates reviews from Google, which shows the potential customer a respected third-parties opinion on this brand's product or service.

The advertisers have also used location extensions and included the nearest o2 store from my location.

Keyword Types

Many first time advertisers have no idea there are different keyword match types. And, as a result, they waste money on irrelevant search phrases that are not part of the keywords listed in the account.

There are 4 main keyword match types:

- Broad
- Phrase
- Exact
- Negative Keywords

Broad Match Keywords

Google Adwords default keyword match type is always set to Broad. If you leave your keywords as Broad match, then Google will show your ads to any search phrase Google thinks is relevant to your keyword.

This means your ads will get more impressions, but you'll likely show ads to irrelevant search phrases that will just waste your budget. So we do not recommend using Broad match keywords.

Phrase Match Keywords

Phrase Keywords will trigger ads when the exact phrase is part of the keyword typed into Google.

For example, if your Phrase match keyword is "chinese restaurant" then your ad will display for "chinese restaurant in nottingham" and "nottingham chinese restaurant"

However, your ad would not display for "chinese food restaurant nottingham" because the phrase "chinese restaurant" is broken up by the word "food."

Phrase match gives you much more control over your ads than Broad match. To change your keyword to Phrase match, simply add quotes around the keyword.

Exact Match Keywords

Exact match simply tells Google to display your ad only when the exact keyword is typed into Google. You'll get the most control with Exact match, but you'll limit your exposure. To set your match type to Exact match, add square brackets around your keywords or select Exact match from the drop in keyword list.

Negative Keywords

By using Negative keywords you have the ability to block phrases from triggering your ads. For example, if you run a chinese restaurant in Nottingham and advertising on the Phrase match keyword, "nottingham restaurant," then you will want to block the keyword "Indian." That way your ads will not display for someone searching for an indian restaurant. To add negative keywords, go to the Keywords tab in your account, scroll down to the bottom, and click on the Negative keyword link or add negatives.

Conversion Tracking

We're almost ready to set up your campaign in AdWords, but there is one final component that a lot of advertisers miss out - conversion tracking. If you skip this step, then you'll never know which keywords and ads are generating sales and which are just losing you money.

Conversion tracking allows you to measure sales generated by your AdWords campaign. More specifically, it helps understand which keywords and ads are generating sales. If some or all of your sales occur online with an e-commerce shopping cart, then conversion tracking is pretty straightforward. Just use the built-in Google AdWords conversion tracking tool to get it installed onto your site. A full guide on conversion tracking can be found on our FAQ's page - www.heartcms.com/faq

Mobile Apps

If you think that mobile apps are solely for big name brands like Nike, Ferrari and Reed.co.uk, you're wrong. More and more small to medium size businesses are following the mobile trend, understanding that an effective mobile strategy involves more than just a mobile-friendly website.

In case you're still unsure why anyone would want to build their own mobile platform, here are the top benefits of having your own iOS and Android app;

Credibility, You Can't Pay For

If a potential customer is considering purchasing from your business and one of your competitors, it's a case of having stronger credibility to secure the customer.

As stated many times in this book, being found online is a tough nut to crack but converting the customer once they find you is another thing.

Having your own mobile app for your business can greatly contribute to your brand awareness and credibility. Finding small businesses with apps are still rare, and this is where you can take a big leap ahead of your competitors. Be the first in your industry to offer a mobile app to your customers.

The more often you can get customers involved with your business, the sooner they will be inclined to use your business. In advertising this is called the "effective frequency", as a rule of thumb, hearing and/or seeing your brand approximately 20 times is what will get you truly noticed (this is why Remarketing works so well).

Improve Customer Engagement

It doesn't matter whether you're selling products or services, your customers need a way to reach out to you. Having your own app enables you to engage with potential customers in real-time and turn those engaged customers into revenue. You customers will also acknowledge that you're an active business and willing to communicate with your audience even if it's about a problem about the product or services that you offer.

Promotions And Push Notifications

A great method of promoting app downloads and customer engagement is by offering free valuable content, coupons and a user friendly experience.

Let's say for example, you run a Restaurant business. You could design and develop an app that includes the following;

- Free Recipies
- Loyalty Scheme (Dine five times, and be rewarded with a free meal)
- Booking system
- Allow customers to leave reviews (and promote them with a 10% voucher for doing so)

By offering great content, customers will be entitled to downloading your free app. Once the customer has downloaded the app, each and every new download will be another person you can market to. You'll be able to send them Push Notifications, which are like text messages but through your app and engage with them in real time.

Case Studies

We have designed and developed three best selling, chart topping number #1 apps on both iOS and Android platforms.

We will share two case studies from the same client to explain how successful these apps have become for this medium size business.

Case Study One: Yiannimize Wrap App

Client : Yiannimize
Web URL : www.yiannimize.com

We briefly touched based on our client that wraps cars for celebrities in our Snapchat section. The car wrapping industry is growing every day, and with lots of companies offering vehicle wrapping solutions, it was our job to make sure Yiannimize stood out from it's competition.

For those of you who are unsure of what vehicle wrapping is, it's when you change the colour of your car using a vinyl wrap instead of having the car repainted. Vehicle wrapping has its benefits over having your car repainted, but that's another story.

So with Yiannimize already having a worldwide fan base, thanks to social media we decided to take it to the next level and develop an App.

What could we do for Yiannimize that would work well, engage customers and set Yiannimize as a leading authority in the vehicle wrapping industry.

If you've not already guessed it, we managed to design and build an app that allowed customers, fans and car fanatics to take photos of their cars and change the appearance and colour of their vehicle.

Before we launched the app, we did our market research and found that there was no other app like this. So we decided to develop the app with the following features;

Select car from garage - This section of the app would allow users to select a pre-loaded vehicle from the app to customise. We introduced this section to the app as we found a lot of our clients followers to be of the younger generation, who may not yet own their own car.

Take a photo of your car - For those car fanatics that do what their car wrapped but want an idea of how their car would look. They can now download this app and see the results before buying the real thing.

Select from gallery - Apps are about creating a user friendly experience, so we decided to allow users to upload images from their smartphones gallery and customise images that were taken in the past.

Request a quote - There was two main objectives for this app, 1) Increase brand awareness and credibility 2) Generate sales. So we decided to include a request a quote feature where app users could send out vehicle details in an e-mail format for our client to reply back with a price.

Tutorials - We decided to add video tutorials to make sure users we're engaging with the app.

We decided to set the app at £1.99 which gave users access to the following features;

- Select from car garage
- Request a quote
- Tutorials

To unlock the main features 'take a photo of your car' and 'select from gallery' the user was promoted with an in-app purchase of a further £1.99.

Now you might be thinking that's £3.98 for the full features of the app - but this case study just proves that outside the box thinking can be a big pay off.

Here are the results after three hours of the app being launched and advertised;

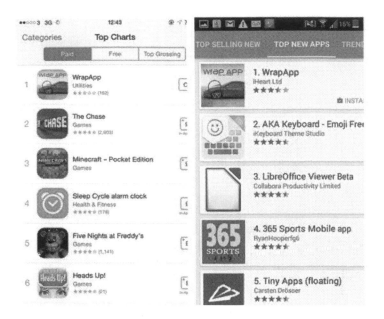

The app soon start trending on both app stores (iOS and Android) and was above the likes of Minecraft and Ellen's world famous Heads Up!.

The app also started to feature on websites and was being reposted by fans, followers and even celebrities. It was also trending on social media with #WrapApp

Enquiries from our clients website and the app itself increased dramatically and lead to sales from all over the country.

The reason for us sharing this case study is to show that any typical everyday business is able to get online exposure by creating an app, regardless of your industry.

To make matters more interesting, the app sold over 20,000 units and has lead to Yiannimize and HeartCMS working together on other apps such as the newly 2016 number #1 racing game (on iOS) - Yiannimize Racing.

Case Study Two : Yiannimize Racing

We're now on our third app for Yiannimize, and the latest one has also hit the number #1 spot on iOS Top Charts, Games and Racing category.

The objective of this app was to raise brand awareness and credibility, so we decided to design and develop a 2D iOS racing game. After performing our market research, we were able to push the game on the app store for £0.69p.

The game managed to reach the iOS 'trending searches' page and beat the likes of Football Manager 2016, Monopoly and Grand Theft Auto: San Andreas.

What Next?

If you like what you've read in this book, we would really appreciate a review on Amazon. It makes a big difference, and we enjoy reading them.

Also, please remember that we are here to answer any questions you might have, We would also be happy to offer our readers a free website report, which will include a check up on everything mentioned in this book.

The next step is to head over to www.heartcms.com/bookoffer, if you haven't already, as you'll be able to claim some free goodies to get you started on your journey.

You'll also be able to claim a free '45 Minute Consultation' with either one of this books authors. To do so please head over to www.heartcms.com/bookoffer

We are here to help, and are happy to offer advice through our website, email or over the phone. Our team of internet marketing experts are the sharpest in the business, and we love nothing more than getting a big fat juicy testimonial from a client we've saved or made a lot of money for.

If you have any feedback, you can contact me personally by email on amen@heartcms.com